Tourism, Regional Development and Public Policy

The tourism industry, as one of the main drivers of creative economy, gains more importance in growth policies both at national and regional levels. However traditional tourism destinations now face a more competitive environment, for an increased number of possible destinations have emerged. This environment is further deepened by an increase in the number of products and services available to the preferences of visitors.

Therefore new tourism policies, unlike traditional strategies, should aim to increase the competitiveness of the local through supporting increased quality of experience and promoting innovation in tourism services. Based on the workshop organized by Regional Studies Association Research Network on "Tourism, Regional Development and Public Policy" in Izmir, Turkey, this book introduces, motivates and examines diversities in the tourism industry from a regional development perspective. The papers in this book cover various case studies from different country experiences. The views expressed in these articles promise to improve our understanding of tourism in a new aspect that goes beyond the mass tourism mentality.

This book was originally published as a special issue of *European Planning Studies.*

Neşe Kumral is Professor of Economics and Head of the Economics Department at Ege University, Turkey.

A. Özlem Önder is Professor of Economics at Ege University, Turkey.

Tourism, Regional Development and Public Policy

Edited by
Neşe Kumral and A. Özlem Önder

Routledge
Taylor & Francis Group

LONDON AND NEW YORK

First published 2012
by Routledge
2 Park Square, Milton Park, Abingdon, Oxon, OX14 4RN

Simultaneously published in the USA and Canada
by Routledge
711 Third Avenue, New York, NY 10017

Routledge is an imprint of the Taylor & Francis Group, an informa business

British Library Cataloguing in Publication Data
A catalogue record for this book is available from the British Library

ISBN13: 978-0-415-69738-5

Typeset in Times New Roman
by Taylor & Francis Books

Disclaimer

The publisher would like to make readers aware that the chapters in this book are referred to as articles as they had been in the special issue. The publisher accepts responsibility for any inconsistencies that may have arisen in the course of preparing this volume for print.

MIX
Paper from
responsible sources
FSC® C004839
www.fsc.org

Printed and bound in Great Britain by the MPG Books Group

Contents

Introduction

NEŞE KUMRAL & A. ÖZLEM ÖNDER

Department of Economics, Ege University, 35100 Izmir, Turkey

The demand for tourism has become more globalized in the last few decades due to the improved technologies of information and communications, better transportation facilities and liberalization of international borders. The traditional tourism destinations now face a more competitive environment, for an increased number of possible destinations have emerged. This environment is further deepened by an increase in the number of products and services available to the preferences of visitors.

The United Nations World Tourism Organization (UNWTO) expects a 4% annual increase in international arrivals for the next 20 years. UNWTO's Tourism 2020 Vision forecasts that the top receiving regions in 2020 will be Europe, East Asia and Pacific and the Americas. This may be taken to imply a not-so-bright future for Africa, the Middle East and South Asia. However, the market shares of the latter group of regions are expected to increase within the same Vision, for these regions are expected to display a tourist arrival growth of 5% annually, which is higher than the expected world average growth rate of 4.1% per year (UNWTO, 2008).

Local suppliers will be able to benefit from this increased mobility as long as they remain competitive vis-à-vis other regions through product differentiation and productivity enhancements. Even though the demand for tourism is becoming global, the supply is inevitably local, since the consumption of goods and services takes place through the interaction of consumers and producers (OECD, 2006, 2008).

What is presented by suppliers is a basket of goods and services that constitute an experience for the visitor. Obviously, the more unique an experience is, the more demanded it will be and the more productive the local supplier will become. Therefore, in order to increase productivity, the suppliers have to innovate by creating new goods and services or coming up with methods to combine traditional goods and services into unique experiences. Such innovative process is highly localized to the geography of the supplier and requires considerable creativity. Hence, local creativity is identified as a major source of productivity and is, therefore, of substantial importance in a locality's global competitiveness (OECD, 2008).

Creative act is a social process and may include tourists as active contributors. Tourism takes on a more creative face as the consumption of creative activities gains a higher portion in the experience presented to the consumer by the local supplier. Such social dimension emphasizes the role of interaction with other people, institutions and other various social structures which may have a previously accumulated stock of knowledge and resources that are usable in the creative process. Then, the quality of experience is a function of creativity and interactivity of the local actors, among which the local suppliers are prominent (Pine and Gilmore, 1999; Richard and Wilson, 2006).

In this context, creativity may contribute to the development of entrepreneurship, enhance an innovative environment and lead to a higher productivity. Therefore, tourism has a unique and little-explored position as one of the main drivers of creativity in the economy, and it has a well-deserved place right next to technology and demand (UNCTAD, 2008).

The tourism industry, as one of the main drivers of creative economy, gains more importance in growth policies both at the national and regional levels. New tourism policies, unlike traditional strategies, should aim to increase the competitiveness of the local through supporting increased quality of experience and promoting innovation in tourism services. However, there exists a limited discussion on this issue in the literature. Therefore, Regional Studies Association Research Network on "Tourism, Regional Development and Public Policy" has planned to organize a series of workshops that aim to examine the diversity of tourism in Europe, and its implication for the socio-economic development and public policy. This issue of "European Planning Studies" contains a selection of five papers from the first workshop of the series. The workshop was hosted by the Ege University in İzmir, Turkey, which was held from 2nd to 4th April 2008. The meeting attracted an audience of around 80 people from different backgrounds including academics, policy-makers and regional administrators as well as students. The programme featured 26 papers. All the papers in this issue were refereed. We thank all the referees for their prompt responses, and we are honoured to be the guest editors for this special issue.

The primary objective of this special issue is to introduce, motivate and examine the diversities in the tourism industry from a regional development perspective. The papers in this issue cover various case study experiences from different countries. The views expressed in these articles promise to improve our understanding of tourism in a new aspect that goes beyond the mass tourism mentality.

In the first paper, Pennie F. Henriksen and Henrik Halkier conducted a case study of a destination management organization, Top of Denmark, in order to determine the factors that drive or hamper the changes in tourism policy from localized marketing towards regional innovation strategies. In their paper, they focus especially on the role of stakeholder networks and knowledge processes in overcoming the spatial fragmentation and product conservatism. They find that the issue of localism has been overcome by establishing and operating Top of Denmark as a network-based body.

The second paper, by Armando Montanari and Barbara Staniscia, deals with the relationship between quality agriculture and wine-and-food tourism on the Apennines of central and southern Italy. They argue that depending on the production methods, food can also become a cultural point of reference, an element of regional development and a touristic resource. Their results suggest that tourism linked to quality agriculture is not only an economic lever, but also a type of contemporary sustainable development. The authors view the process to be at its initial phases and suggest from bottom-up approach that it needs further public support.

The third paper by Craig Webster, Bernard Musyck, Stelios Orphanides and David Jacobson examines the willingness of the professionals in Greek Cypriot tourism to cooperate with their Turkish Cypriot counterparts in the industry. They argue that there is clear evidence that the Greek Cypriot hotel managers are unlikely at present to cooperate with the Turkish Cypriot counterparts. On the other hand, the Greek Cypriot tour operators and tourist agencies are willing to collaborate with the other side. They conclude that the tourism agencies and tour operators are the most important actors in terms of fostering cooperation between tourism professionals in the two entities in Cyprus.

The last two contributions come form Turkey and are related to the tourism industry in the Aegean Region and Izmir, respectively. Firstly, Yaprak Gülcan, Yeşim Kuştepeli, Sedef Akgüngör's paper focuses on the significance of the tourism sector in the Aegean Region in comparison with the rest of the nation. The results of their location-quotient estimations suggest that the Aegean Region is highly specialized in the tourism industry. The findings verify that the value added created by the hotels of the Aegean region is higher than the country average. By using an econometric model, the study illustrates that the public investments in tourism have been the significant tools to create higher value added in the region between 1995 and 2001. Finally, Özlem Önder, Aykan Candemir, Neşe Kumral examine the determinants of the demand for international tourism in Izmir, using time-series data. The findings suggest that the prices and income of the tourist generating countries are the main determinants of the demand for tourism. The local factors related to Izmir's level of development and the transportation of the public capital stock have no significant effect. The authors argue that the government should encourage alternative forms of tourism development besides mass tourism.

References

OECD (Organisation for Economic Co-operation and Development) (2006) *Innovation and Growth in Tourism* (Paris: OECD).

OECD (Organisation for Economic Co-operation and Development) (2008) *Tourism in OECD Countries 2008: Trends and Policies* (Paris: OECD).

Pine, B. J. & Gilmore, J. H. (1999) *The Experience Economy* (Boston, MA: Harvard University Press).

Richards, G. & Wilson, J. (2006) Developing creativity in tourist experiences: A solution to the serial reproduction of culture? *Tourism Management*, 27(6), pp. 1209–1223.

UNCTAD (United Nations Conference on Trade and Development & United Nations Development Programme) (2008) *Creative Economy Report 2008, The challenge of Assessing the Creative Economy: Towards Informed Policy-Making* (Switzerland/USA: UNCTAD).

UNWTO (World Tourism Organization) (2008) *Tourism Highlights, 2008 Edition, UNWTO* (Madrid, Spain: UNWTO). Available at www.unwto.org/facts/eng/highlights.htm (accessed February 2009).

From Local Promotion Towards Regional Tourism Policies: Knowledge Processes and Actor Networks in North Jutland, Denmark

PENNIE F. HENRIKSEN & HENRIK HALKIER

Tourism Research Unit, Aalborg University, Denmark

ABSTRACT *Public policies promoting the development of tourist destinations, not least in North-western Europe, have traditionally focused on attracting more tourists through local promotional activities, but in many localities these have now been supplemented by strategies that attempt to change the tourist product on offer, often operating at the regional level, and thus, tourism policies have changed with regard to scale, aims and instruments. Research on the tourism policy has mainly centred on the difficulties inherent in destination development with regard to orchestrating changes in the wide raft of services, typically provided by small local firms, that make up the tourist experience, while less attention has been given to an important prerequisite for these new, product-development strategies, namely the process of policy change from local promotion towards regional tourism policies, despite the potential difficulties involved in shifting geographical scales of governance and adopting a more risky focus on new types of visitors. The aim of this article is to investigate the factors that drive or hamper the tourism policy change from localized marketing towards regional innovation strategies, focusing especially on the role of stakeholder networks and knowledge processes in overcoming spatial fragmentation and product conservatism. Adopting an institutionalist perspective, an in-depth case study of a destination management organization, "Top of Denmark", situated at the tip of one of northern Europe's prime locations for seaside tourism, is undertaken in order to identify factors that drive or hamper the policy change from localized marketing towards regional, product-development initiatives. This article concludes that the issue of localism has been effectively addressed by establishing and operating as a network-based body where individual stakeholders are mutually dependant on the specific capacities of their partners, a consensual style of decision-making is prevailing, and a division of labour has been established that engages local actors in destination-wide tasks while at the same time enabling them to maintain close links with small tourism businesses in their area. Both in the emergence and in the redevelopment of the organization, the internal wish for change has clearly been stimulated by extra-destinational incentives, but the* *perceived success of the early, joint-marketing activities has clearly made the current focus on product-development activities easier.*

1. Introduction

Public policies promoting the development of tourist destinations, not least in North-western Europe, have traditionally focused on attracting more tourists, primarily through the promotional activities of individual localities. Although promotion is still a conspicuous element in tourism development, such "boosterist" activities have, in many destinations, been replaced by, or at least supplemented by, strategies that attempt to change the tourist product on offer, typically in order to make it more environmentally sustainable and/or more appealing to more discerning visitors willing to pay for quality and novelty (Hall, 2008). Partly inspired by the growing salience of the regional level with regard to the innovation policies, these new-model tourism policies have often operated at the regional rather than at the local level, and thus, scale, aims and instruments have changed when moving from local promotion towards regional, product-development policies within tourism.

Research on tourism policy has mainly centred on these new strategies for destination development (cf. the literature review below), in particular the difficulties inherent in attempts to orchestrate changes that involve a combination of very different services—transport, hospitality, attractions, activities—many of which are typically provided by small local firms. Less attention has, however, been given to an important prerequisite for these new, product-development strategies, namely the process of policy change from local promotion towards regional tourism policies, and this is rather surprising. Not only does the general path-dependency within the public policy make continuity the "default option" (Hogwood, 1992; Hood, 1994), but the specific challenges involved in bringing about this particular policy change would also appear to be significant. On the one hand, changing the geographical scale through collaboration with neighbouring localities in order to achieve greater impact in the market place can clearly be complicated when these localities have traditionally been construed as competitors. On the other hand, moving from a promotion-based strategy, in an attempt to increase the use of existing facilities, towards an innovation-based one where the destination starts competing in new markets for tourists looking for different experiences is clearly risky and much more demanding in terms of knowledge about the international markets and the capabilities of local firms to change. In short, the dual pressures of localism and short-termism are likely to be the major impediments for the introduction of product-development-oriented policies for tourist destinations.

The aim of this article is to investigate the factors that drive or hamper tourism policy change from localized marketing towards regional innovation strategies, focusing especially on the role of stakeholder networks and knowledge processes in overcoming spatial fragmentation and product conservatism. The text proceeds in three steps. First the existing literature on tourism policy is reviewed in order to re-conceptualize the issues from an institutionalist perspective. Then the design of the empirical analysis is outlined, combining elements of network analysis with a knowledge biography approach for an in-depth case study of a destination management organization (DMO) that, reputedly, has been relatively effective in addressing localism and short-termism, namely the Top of Denmark (ToD) at the heart—or rather tip—of one of northern Europe's prime locations for seaside tourism. Finally, the main part of the article presents the empirical findings from an in-depth study of the emergence and development of the ToD, focusing on the role of stakeholders within the network and the knowledge processes between them. On the basis of this it should be possible to identify factors that drive or hamper the policy change from localized marketing towards regional, product-development initiatives.

2. Tourism and Public Policy: Towards a Reconceptualization

Academic research on the tourism policy is still relatively sparse (Hall, 2008), and amidst a gradually growing body of rather descriptive case studies, the attempts to develop typologies and conceptual frameworks have remained fairly basic. In an oft-quoted article, Fayos-Solá (1996) suggested the existence of three generations of tourism policy:

- First-generation policies focused on increasing the volume of activity in order to maximize the income (often referred to as "boosterism").
- Second-generation policies attempted to expand tourism as an industry through subsidies, promotion and regulation (spatial planning, environmental regulation)
- Third-generation policies aimed at increasing the competitiveness through increased quality and efficiency in service delivery.

Although these strategies are neither seen as mutually exclusive nor necessarily sequential, it is, however, also clear that what this typology amounts to is a series of ideal-type policy paradigms with a built-in (vague) assumption of progress over time, based primarily on the different types of expansive objectives for tourism destinations, ranging from first-generation "more of the same" via second-generation "more of most" to third-generation "more of the best".

While this generational typology may have an intuitive heuristic appeal, its usefulness in empirical analysis of tourism policy is more doubtful, because the same goals may be pursued in very different ways and, indeed, the link between the aims and methods may be as tenuous as in other areas of the public policy (Hogwood & Gunn, 1986). More multi-dimensional perspectives on tourism policy can be found in the studies of strategies promoting innovation in the tourist product, where a recurring theme in the growing literature on tourism policy at destination-level is the importance of networking (e.g. Jamal & Getz, 1995; Saxena, 2005; Dredge, 2006; Cawley *et al.*, 2007) and the inspiration from the general literature on policy networks is evident (e.g. Thorelli, 1986; Rhodes & Marsh, 1992; Cooke & Morgan, 1998). Most studies of the emerging new-model network initiatives tend to emphasize the difficulties involved in network creation, with recurring references to local parochialism, public–private distrust and internal competition being factors often hampering destination development, and from a regional development perspective this is perhaps less surprising because tourist destinations would appear to be different to the much-hyped networking clusters in both high-tech and more traditional industries (see e.g. Saxenian, 1985; Bellini & Pasquini, 1998; Cooke, 2001; Ache, 2002; Newlands, 2003; Steiner & Ploder, 2008). As suggested by Hjalager's seminal contribution (Hjalager, 2000), although a large number of service providers are located within a tourist destination, external firms such as tour operators or transport providers often play a central role, free-riding with regard to the participation in collective endeavours is often endemic and the unstable nature of tourism SMEs both in terms of ownership and employment makes the building of trust difficult. Still, some destinations could potentially function as clusters, provided that high levels of networking and knowledge-sharing take place so that a combination of competition and collaboration characterize the relationship between the firms and organizations providing services to tourists, and this places the institutionalized networks and knowledge processes to centre stage in public policies for the tourism innovation and destination development.

In order to capture the complexities of the processes of strategic change in tourist destinations in a systematic manner, an approach inspired by an institutionalist perspective on the public policy and policy networks (Halkier, 2006) will be taken, focusing on the key characteristics of different types of tourism policy on the one hand, and those of the policy networks in which they are embedded on the other.

In terms of the strategies for tourism development, the analysis will focus on the specific changes sought by the public policy and distinguish between the two main components producing the tourist experience, namely the various services that contribute to the experience on the one hand, and the promotion of these services to potential customers on the other. As illustrated by Table 1, this results in four basic variants of tourism policy which may of course coexist in any given destination, but still have very different implications both for stakeholders within the destination and for the tourists that are likely to be attracted to the destination. In an "on-site information strategy", neither the external promotion nor the tourist experience change, and hence, providing local information services through the tourist offices—something that can be achieved relatively easily by small subscriptions from private stakeholders and local authority support—will at best have a word-of-mouth effect in relation to friends and family of existing tourists. In a "marketing-oriented strategy", the existing services are promoted to a wider audience, but apart from the financial contributions, little is required of stakeholders within the destination, and the expected outcome is the better use of existing capacities through a greater inflow of tourists similar to those already holidaying in the destination. In a "product development strategy" the emphasis is on changing particular services that contribute to the tourist experience—something that requires investment, knowledge and new procedures in individual organizations—in order to make them more attractive to potential tourists. The more comprehensive and widespread the product development is, the greater the need for concurrently refocusing promotional efforts and engaging in a "rebranding strategy" that repositions the destination in the competition for visitors, involving coordinated efforts with regard to both product and promotion and hence a considerable element of risk. In short, the key challenge in tourism policy revolves around coordination of the activities of a large and heterogeneous group of stakeholders, but depending on the strategy chosen, different coordination issues arise: localism may hamper the attempts to achieve greater external visibility through joint-promotion efforts, short-termism may impede product development not least if other actors

Table 1. A typology of tourism policies

Tourist experience	Promotion	
	Continuity	Change
Continuity	On-site information strategy	Marketing strategy
Change	Product development strategy	Rebranding strategy

are not trusted to follow suit—and a comprehensive strategy for destination rebranding are of course challenging on both counts. Policy change, in other words, may be difficult to achieve even in situations where many actors agree that in principle it is much needed.

With regard to the policy networks, the main focus and degree of detail varies in the existing literature (Halkier & Damborg, 1997), but common central features are resource dependencies and interaction patterns, and hence the analysis follows Halkier (2006, Chapter 3) in focusing on the network relations with regard to four key policy resources—authority, finance, information and organization—and the role of individual actors as more or less proactive or reactive and hence with varying degrees of influence on the agenda within the network. Given the importance attached to learning and knowledge exchange in policy development in general and policy networks in particular, the analysis will focus in particular on the knowledge dynamics within the processes of strategic change, with emphasis given to the nature of knowledge agency, the geography of knowledge exchanges and the transformation of knowledge through interaction (cf. Crevoisier *et al.*, 2007):

- The relationship between "use and generation" of knowledge, i.e. what kind of knowledge is used and generated by which actors within the destination and hence, the extent to which the local destination has the capacity to procure or produce knowledge for policy development.
- The relationship between "proximity and distance", i.e. the extent to which knowledge interactions take place with actors inside and outside the destination and hence, the extent to which policy change is being informed by local or extra-destinational concerns.
- The relationship between "mobility and anchoring" of knowledge, i.e. the extent to which different knowledges are being transformed by being brought together either within or outside the destination and hence the ability of local actors to influence policy agendas within and outside their destination.

Taken together these three dimensions of knowledge dynamics, in conjunction with the general points about resources and actors' roles within the network, should be able to illuminate the development of tourism policies in Denmark's most northerly seaside destination by establishing to what extent and through what means the issues of localism and short-termism have been addressed when attempting to move from local promotion towards regional, product-development policies in order to reposition the destination on the increasingly competitive market for tourism experiences.

3. Study Methods

The destination management organization "ToD"[1] has been chosen to provide a framework for the empirical research. ToD is interesting as a case study of the process of change, specifically the development of destination-level tourism policy, because not only has it managed to overcome localism and develop a common promotional platform, but recently it has also been chosen by the national tourism organization VisitDenmark to participate in a high-profile development project concerning all-year tourism, something which clearly shifted the policy focus towards developing the product offered by the destination. The case study, therefore, focuses on two periods (cf. Henriksen, 2008): the emergence of ToD (1989–1996) and the current redevelopment of the destination

Table 2. Organizations central to tourism development in the ToD destination

Organization	Established	Sponsored	Function
Foundation Top of Denmark (FToD)	1989	Nine local tourism associations	Joint information services and marketing
Destination Top of Denmark (ToD)	1996	FToD and nine (after the 2007 local government reform three) local authorities	Joint marketing and product development
VisitDenmark (previously Danish Tourist Board)	1992	Danish central government	International marketing and product development, sponsor of the national all-year tourism project from 2008
VisitDenmark	2007	Danish central government	Development of marketing, products organization and competences, sponsors of the national and the regional all-year tourism projects from 2008, respectively
VisitNordjylland (VNJ)	2007	North Jutland region	

(2007–2015), and in both phases, resource dependencies and actor roles will be analysed, and particular emphasis will be given to examining the knowledge dynamics in the development of the DMO. Table 2 provides an overview of the most important organizations and their role in tourism development in the northern-most part of Denmark.

During the winter 2008, 12 in-depth semi-structured face-to-face interviews were carried out with the actors on destination management level, i.e. ToD's board members, the administrative core, local heads of tourism within the destination and the manager of the regional tourism development organization VisitNordjylland (VNJ). Because ToD is a network organization with a decentralized structure, individual interviewees may appear in more than one of the three groups and thus, represent more than one perspective on the organization as well as different types of knowledge regarding tourism development—an obvious example of this is the CEO of ToD who also acts as a local head of tourism and is a member of the board—so that all in all a comprehensive coverage of key actors has been achieved for the period in which the DMO has existed. The data have been generated using a so-called knowledge biography method developed as part of the *EURODITE* project, where the objective of the knowledge biography is to grasp the entire set of events, actors and flows that form the knowledge dynamics needed to organize a change in organization, product and/or process (Butzin *et al.*, 2007). The analysis focuses in particular on three dimensions of knowledge dynamics—generation/use, proximity/distance, and mobility/anchorage—and attempts to position these in different knowledge contexts: the firm/organization itself, the markets and networks in which it operates and the wider environment in terms of governance, knowledge institutions, society and culture. In covering these different knowledge contexts, the interview questions strive to uncover which knowledge use/generated and related to which events, who are the players involved, where are they located (local, regional, national, international) and what kind of special interactions does occur and finally, what policies at different administrative scales play a direct or indirect role in the firm knowledge dynamics. Therefore, the questions span from focusing on the individual respondents role and responsibilities within the organization, what types of knowledge the respondents use/ generated as part of their daily work routines in the specific phase analysed to question regarding which external factors (political, social, economic, markets, etc.) influences the given development phase and the knowledge dynamics characterising it. Given our interest in the policy development over time, we sought information relating to past events, and limitation did occur due to respondents not remembering in detail for instance specific knowledge use, collaborative partners or information sources, etc. Nonetheless, the experience was that what one respondent could not remember another one could, and as the empirical research went on it proved that the organizational structure on management level reflecting the respondents' responsibility areas was strongly connected to the type of knowledge they knew something about, remembered and in what detail.

4. Tourism Policy and Knowledge Dynamics in the ToD

This section presents an in-depth case of the development of tourism policy in the North Jutland high-profile seaside destination and its DMO ToD. After having briefly introduced ToD as a tourist destination and its network based DMO, this section proceeds by discussing first the knowledge use and generation, then the proximity and distance in knowledge interaction, and finally, the mobility and anchoring of knowledge.

4.1 Destination TOD and its DMO Network

Destination TOD consists of the three northernmost Danish municipalities, it has around 130,000 inhabitants, and tourism is of major importance to the local economy, even more so in the wake of major industrial closures in recent years. The tourism sector in TOD turns over €300 million and contributes with 4360 full-time jobs in 2004 or 6.9% of total employment in the destination (Toppen af Danmark, 2007b; Arbejdsmarkedsstyrelsen, 2008). Although there has been an overall decline in the number of overnight stays in the North Jutland region, the destination has also experienced a positive economic development in the last decade as a result of the increasing number of high-spending Danish and Norwegian tourists at the expense of especially German visitors (Toppen af Danmark, 2007a). The keywords which ToD uses to describe the destination's tourism experience are relaxation, experiences and activities in authentic, safe and scenic surroundings (Toppen af Danmark, 2006). From a tourism development perspective, the sea, the sandy beaches and nature in general are the destination's main attractions; with 250 km of sandy coastline, seaside tourism is the most popular form of tourism in the destination, supported by cultural experiences such as small arts and craft businesses, and a wide range of active tourism attractions such as golf courses and indoor skiing, and with daily ferry connections from Norway and Sweden and uncongested motorways to the rest of Denmark and northern Germany, accessibility from the main markets is easy.

The story of ToD began in 1989 as the "Foundation Top of Denmark" (FToD) when nine local tourism associations—consisting of local business actors and interested citizens—formed a collaborative network with the main purpose of developing a joint computerized reservation system for holiday houses within the destination, the rental of which was administrated by the local tourist information offices. The setting up of the FToD network was financially supported by the European Fishery Action programme for a three-year period (1989–1991) with the purpose of developing the tourism sector by applying, in the case of FToD, information technology and (very basic) joint marketing efforts in the form of a common logo. In 1992–1993, FToD decided to buy advertisement space so that tourists could see the geographical coherence of the local areas within the destination, supplementing the small, black-and-white paper pamphlets each of the nine tourist information bureaus used to market their local holiday houses, and in 1995 FToD received additional European subsidies for the purpose of creating a joint brochure for the entire destination and prolonging the tourism season. Despite the latter, it appears that joint marketing activities were the main priority of the organization's activities.

Especially since the mid-1990s, prolonging the season has been a strategic priority for ToD. Recently, VisitDenmark launched a major initiative to develop all-year tourism in coastal destinations. In November 2006, ToD applied to take part in the development project, and in June 2007, ToD was chosen by VisitDenmark as one out of seven so-called super all-year tourism destinations, and thus, ToD is redeveloping as a tourism destination by taking part in a national project running till 2015. In parallel with this VisitNordjylland, the regional tourism development organization for the wider North Jutland region, started a parallel project with the regional tourism stakeholders with the purpose of identifying the possibilities of developing all-year tourism in the region as a whole. At the time when the research was conducted, the all-year tourism project was in an early stage of concept development, wherein the main challenge is to successfully prolong the season through product and marketing development, and ensuring the support of relevant stakeholders within the destination, both traditional tourism actors and from other relevant service providers. In other words, a tourism policy initiative that would seem to belong to the rebranding category because it aimed to develop both new products and new promotional strategies in order to reposition the destination in the market for tourism experiences.

Concurrent with these changes in tourism policy, the characteristics of the ToD network were also changing. In the early years, the organizational structure and actor composition of the network changed as a result of incentives established through the national tourism policy. In 1992, the Danish Government invited public and private actors to cooperate across the existing administrative boundaries in order to establish the regional and destina-tion organizations, and in 1994, the Danish Government furthermore decentralized funds to tourism development (Kvistgaard, 2006). Accordingly, the DMO network was reorgan-ized, became a limited company, and changed its name to "ToD" in 1996, becoming a partnership between the nine local tourism associations (FToD) and the then nine munici-palities which the tourism associations represented. ToD's main challenge in the emer-gence phase was ensuring tourism actors' willingness to collaborate and set aside the localist self-interest in order to strengthen the competitive advantage of the individual tourism actors and the destination as a whole. Today, as a result of the structural reform of Danish sub-national government in January 2007 which greatly reduced the number of sub-national entities and redistributed tasks between the regional and local levels, ToD is a partnership between the three municipalities of Frederikshavn, Hjørring and Læsø, as illustrated in Figure 1, together with the tourism associations in FToD. Within the destination, 700 businesses are estimated to have some connection to tourism, and of these ToD has contact with around 400 in relation to development projects and marketing efforts (Toppen af Danmark, 2006). The organization is a collaborative

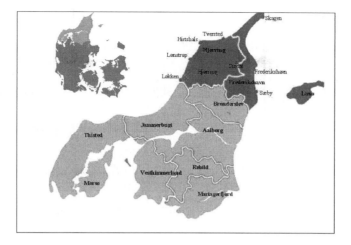

Figure 1. Destination TOD
Note: Destination TOD is indicated with dark grey, and tourist information offices indicated
with circles.

network with a decentralized structure, and in terms of authority and financial resources the
DMO consists of mutually dependant stakeholders: funding stems from local authority
taxation, membership fees from the tourist associations, and business income from
holiday-house rental, and as a voluntary network, each partner could in theory withdraw,
although this is unlikely to happen as long as ToD continues to operate in an inclusive and
consensual manner and is able to deliver results in terms of developing tourism within the
destination. Moreover, also in terms of organizational resources, the dependency appears
to be mutual in the sense that each of the three key actor groups appears to have distinct and
complementary roles:

- The local heads of tourism (all together nine, still reflecting the situation before the 2007
  structural reform) have responsibility for tourism in their individual geographical areas
  and its contribution to the development of the destination as a whole. Furthermore, it is
  their responsibility to secure local political influence, and thus, functioning as the private
  tourism actors' voice in the development of the destination. Within the DMO, each head
  of tourism functions as chairman in at least one of ToD's sub-committees, thereby
  having responsibility for that specific area of development for the whole destination,
  for instance competency development, IT development or marketing.
- The purpose of the administrative core of the DMO is to solve a number of coordinating
  and administrative tasks regarding development projects and undertake the day-to-day
  management of ToD, including provision of administrative support for ToD's governing
  board. Additional administrative tasks are solved in collaboration with the tourism
  information bureaus.
- The board acts as a link between municipal politics and administration on the one hand
  and the practical and strategic activities of ToD on the other, and this involves evaluat-
  ing the overall development of tourism within the destination, oversee strategies and
  implementation, proposing the annual budget proposal for the DMO, and ensuring

that the development plans of ToD are consistent with other public policies, e.g. planning and environment protection. The three mayors of the destination and the CEO are members of ToD's board ex officio. Additionally, the board consists of two municipal council members and three tourism association representatives from FToD.

It is this organizational setting in which destination-level tourism policy gradually appears to have been able to address localism and short-termism among the tourism actors, and in the following, the knowledge processes involved in the development of the DMO will be analysed in order to identify drivers and impediments in what appears to be a comprehensive policy changes, from local tourism promotion towards regional cluster policies. For each of the three dimensions of knowledge dynamics—use/generation, proximity/distance, mobility/anchoring—the role of each of the three key actor groups within the DMO network—the local heads of tourism, the administrative core and the board—will be established, both in the emergence phase of ToD and in the current redevelopment phase.

4.2 *Knowledge Use and Generation in Tourism Policy Development*

The distinction between use and generating of knowledge is important because knowledge generation is an investment in resource development for future economic development and can be assumed to provide an important input to developing strategies specific to ToD as a tourist destination through gathering, processing and interpretation of knowledge, where use of knowledge can be categorized as the application of existing knowledge nonetheless also contributing to the development of economic development. The research conducted has shown that each three actor group within ToD have specific areas of strength regarding knowledge use and generation.

In the emergence phase, the local heads of tourism use knowledge mainly with regard to promoting the destination and optimising services. With regard to the development of ToD's organizational structure, the local heads of tourism's own collaboration experiences were used and contrasted with previous experiences from other DMOs which seemed to suggest that a centralized top-down structure was not a workable solution in a Danish context. At the same time, the local heads of tourism have a rich generation of knowledge in the emergence phase, coordinating information on the total tourism experience together with developing and handling knowledge needed in order to function as chairmen in the ToD sub-committees. The administrative core has a high use of knowledge in the emergence phase, especially specific technical knowledge with respect to the organizational structure, economy and overall development of the organization along with taking previous experiences from other Danish DMOs into account when developing the organizational structure of the DMO. Though not at the same level as their usage of existing knowledge, the administrative core also generate knowledge, in the emergence phase, working with the local heads of tourism in defining strategies and interpreting administrative and technical knowledge when pioneering partnership between the public and private tourism actors. The board activities are based on the knowledge supplied from the administrative core, but the board also use more general political knowledge about tourism and socio-economic development which, in many of the board members' cases, is knowledge obtained though their jobs as politicians, engaging in political networks.

Compared with the emergence of ToD, the redevelopment phase displays a noticeable difference, especially in the use and generation of knowledge by the local heads of tourism and the administrative core. In relation to the development of all-year tourism, the local heads of tourism and the board both have minimum use of knowledge, due to the simple fact that it is the administrative core that functions as the overall coordinator of the project. Traditionally, the development of various projects have been assigned to a sub-committee within ToD, but it appears that the extensive scope of the all-year tourism project has resulted in specific resources being invested in developing this project in order to comply with the tight timeframe and at the same time maintain the quality of other tasks and initiatives both on destination and local level. Knowledge used by the administrative core is primarily general knowledge concerning product and market development together with the knowledge on innovative thinking and network building. As opposed to the emergence phase, knowledge concerning markets and products are examined through analysis, and for the first time, concrete systematic analysis is conducted by ToD.

All in all, the changing patterns of use and generation of knowledge within ToD would seem to reflect its changing strategies and organization, as summarized by Table 3. On the one hand, a shift in terms of strategy from a product-based, marketing-oriented phase where knowledge was primarily generated at the local level through close contacts with private service providers to a more market-oriented strategy where the administrative core plays a central role in generating knowledge about the new markets. On the other hand, it is also noticeable that this shift towards more centralized knowledge generation would appear to be widely accepted, partly due to the building of trust that has taken place during the emergence phase, and partly in order to safeguard existing local and joint activities that are clearly seen as valuable.

4.3 Proximity and Distant Knowledge Interactions in ToD

This section explores the geographical characteristics of knowledge interactions, i.e. knowledge flows within the destination, and between ToD and actors in the wider North Jutland region and beyond. Concerning the knowledge dimension of proximity and distant knowledge interactions, the spatial distribution of knowledge flows for the three key actor groups with regard to the emergence and redevelopment of the DMO are examined, i.e. the frequency and volume of knowledge interactions with actors outside the region of North Jutland and how knowledge flows within the ToD network and the North Jutland region.

Table 3. Use and generation of knowledge in ToD

	Local heads of tourism	Administrative core
Use	(1) Knowledge about organization, marketing and service optimization	(1) Knowledge about organization and marketing
	(2) Knowledge about all-year tourism project	(2) Organizational and product knowledge
Generation	(1) Product knowledge	(1) Knowledge about strategy
	(2) Limited knowledge production due to internal task allocation	(2) Market intelligence

Note: (1) Emergence phase; (2) Redevelopment phase.

The knowledge exchanges of ToD are many and of different character. Knowledge is exchanged through direct knowledge channels, such as network meetings, internal seminars, intranet and committee meetings, as well as through distant knowledge channels such as phone, internet and students doing internships. The internal knowledge interaction through daily contacts and weekly meetings appeared to be the most important forms of knowledge interaction, together with participation in various networks. The intense internal interchanges result in actors knowing each other's professional and, to some degree, personal strengths, competences and weaknesses, and thus, it helps build the network as the actors know the resources available as well as it strengthens trust between the actors. In addition to this, the various external networks which the three identified actors groups participate in present an opportunity for ToD to interact with actors from the regional and national levels. This is of significant political importance because it gives ToD actors the opportunity to influence decisions regarding tourism development, especially on the regional level, but also creates opportunities for additional networking and inspiration, even occasionally from international sources.

The knowledge interactions of ToD in the emergence phase generally occurred internally in the organization as a part of the process of developing network-based collaboration and activities. The local heads of tourism mainly directed their interactions towards private tourism actors in their local area in order to ensure their approval of and participation in DMO activities and acquire information useful for the mapping and coordination of the total tourism experience as input to joint marketing activities. Similarly, the administrative core also focused internally as their main task consisted of organizing and structuring administrative issues concerning the organization's emergence. Due to the political representation in the board, this group of actors appears to have much interaction with other regional actors, as a result of their participation in various political networks and boards. At this point in time (1989–1996), no tradition for sector-specific networks existed, and thus networking between tourism actors was of a more informal nature. With regard to the distant knowledge interactions in the emergence phase, the local heads of tourism and the board have similar positions, although the frequency and type of exchanges differ. The local heads of tourism have extra-regional knowledge interaction in their communication with national and international tourism destinations and external experts with the purpose of obtaining new knowledge and inspiration regarding primarily marketing and service development—and, of course, direct interactions with tourists visiting the tourism information bureaus which create informal information about tourists' needs and perceptions. The board's extra-regional knowledge interactions mainly happened through the political representatives' participation in extra-regional network, but due to the administrative core's central role in coordinating the administrative, financial and legal aspects of the organization's emergence, the necessity to retrieve guidelines and specific technical knowledge was strong and prompted intense interactions with the legal advisors and national association specializing in municipal issues.

In the current redevelopment phase, especially the administrative core has experienced a significant change in the geography of their knowledge interactions. The local heads of tourism and the board generally do not participate in the planning and strategic development phase of the all-year project, as it is the administrative core that acts as the overall coordinator of the project, and therefore, the heads of tourism's current knowledge interactions within the region can be described as relatively poor with regard to this specific project. But as prolonging the tourism season has been a development issue for many years within the destination, they still have regional knowledge interaction with private tourism actors in the mapping of attractions. Actors from the board now participate in a number of regional tourism networks, alongside networks focusing on other sectors of development, such as education and technology, and it appears that the board, to some degree, represent the glue between other regional political tourism actors and ToD, ensuring political influence on both the destination and the regional level. As a result of being among the vanguard in VisitDenmark's all-year tourism project, the administrative core has engaged in very rich knowledge interactions on the regional level with VisitNord-jylland and other public bodies as a part of the regional initiative to extend all-year tourism beyond the ToD area. Moreover, the administrative core has initiated collaboration and network activities with non-traditional tourism actors such as the fishing industry with the purpose of involving new actors, hopefully developing the total tourism experience so that it has a wider appeal in terms of experiences, seasonality and tourists, and thereby strengthens the business and socio-economic development in the destination generally.

In contrast to this, the extra-regional knowledge interactions of the local heads of tourism in the redevelopment phase are now limited to their contact with tourist visiting the tourism information bureaus, generating an informal form of market intelligence. Also, the board has limited extra-regional knowledge interactions, primarily through the CEO's activities as a key player in the administrative core. The administrative core, in contrast, has very rich knowledge interactions outside the destination due to VisitDenmark and VisitNordjylland's involvement in the project, as both tiers of tourism policy above ToD demand knowledge sharing and collaboration of project participants, including study trips and international seminars. To what extent ToD would spend resources on knowledge interactions with the public tourism actors from the regional and national levels, if it was not a requirement for project participation, would, however, be good to know, as the lack of time and personnel resources is seen to be barriers in this respect.

As summarized in Table 4, the overall impression of the geography of ToD's knowledge interactions is, therefore, exchanges within the destination itself or the wider region of North Jutland clearly dominate, while the significant increase in interaction with more distant partners has, at least initially, been driven by the resources and demands from the external sponsors.

4.4 *Mobility and Anchoring of Knowledge in ToD*

The purpose of this section is to analyse how knowledge coming from the outside is put to use by ToD, and how, in return, the DMO influences external knowledges. The analysis

Table 4. Proximity and distance knowledge relations in ToD

	Local heads of tourism	Administrative core
Proximity	(1) Local firms, ToD network	(1) ToD network
	(2) Local firms, ToD network	(2) ToD network, non-tourism firms
Distance	(1) Incoming tourists	(1) External advisers
	(2) Incoming tourists	(2) VisitDenmark, VNJ, external consultants, other DMOs

Note: (1) Emergence phase; (2) Redevelopment phase.

has so far shown that the three key actor groups within ToD obtain and employ various types of knowledge coming from sources of both a local, regional, national and international character. In the light of these findings, this section will focus on the ways in which knowledge mobility, i.e. the movement of knowledge from one spatial context to another, influences the knowledges involved. Hence, the following focuses on the interaction between regional and external knowledge for each of the three actor groups, i.e. the extent to which mobile knowledge is transformed through the interaction with regional knowledge and the extent to which regional knowledge is transformed through the interaction with external knowledge.

The local heads of tourism were the key initiators of the destination collaboration network, and they have, since the emergence, been the glue that connects the private tourism actors and ToD, especially by communicating ToD's strategies and plans of action through meetings and network sessions on the local level. In the emergence phase there appears to have been a great deal of mobile knowledge entering the local heads of tourism's knowledge sphere, for instance through seminars, daily contact with each other local heads, newsletter and through the private tourism actors, and locally the local heads of tourism spread and contextualize the knowledge from the international, national and regional level throughout the destination; thus, functioning as the private tourism actors' main source of knowledge regarding destination development. Additionally, as the local heads of tourism had, and still have, a strong connection and a rich information flow with private tourism actors, they have a clear idea about their products and challenges, and this information allows the former to mould and modify both the regional and the extra-regional knowledge so that it fits the local needs and the destination TOD as a whole. Another example of the local heads of tourism's contextualization of extra-regional knowledge is their use of previous experiences from other Danish DMO concerning the organizational structure and management of tourism development. Generally, the heads of tourism appear to have been very proactive concerning the development of the destination by obtaining new knowledge when needed.

Due to the responsibilities of the administrative core in the emergence phase, apart from participating in the contextualization of organizational experiences from other DMOs, this group of actors also transmitted the external knowledge unaltered to ToD in the emergence phase, especially the specific legal knowledge that could not be moulded or modified but simply had to be complied with. In the case of the board, it appears that there is a limited interaction between the regional and mobile knowledge in the emergence phase, as the main focus of the board is on the administrative core, i.e. internal knowledge of the organization. Generally, the internal knowledge flows are very rich within ToD and these are also moulded and modified to match the needs of the local areas within the destination, and this would seem to reflect the organization's decentralized network structure while developing its tourism management strategy. However, even in the emergence phase, ToD can be said to have sparked the regional and extra-regional knowledge dynamics, for instance through the tourism policy practitioners and knowledge institutions contacting the DMO to learn more about the ToD experience, although this only took place in a reactive and unsystematic way.

The local heads of tourism and the board have not changed much when comparing the emergence phase and the present redevelopment phase of the destination, reflecting the fact that the administrative core is in charge and thus, the main proactive force in the current stage of the all-year tourism project. However, the increasingly common

Table 5. Anchoring and mobility of knowledge in ToD

	Local heads of tourism	Administrative core
Anchoring	(1) Contextualization of organizational knowledge	(1) Transmission of legal advice, contextualization of organizational knowledge
	(2) Contextualization of product development knowledge	(2) Contextualization of organizational knowledge and market intelligence
Mobility	(1) Mobilization of local product knowledge	(1) Inspiration of other DMOs
	(2) Mobilization of local product knowledge	(2) Coaching of other DMOs

Note: (1) Emergence phase; (2) Redevelopment phase.

practice of establishing regional networks within tourism and other industries means that the two actor groups have generally developed a stronger degree of interaction between regional and mobile knowledge. The administrative core functions as the key interpreter and distributor of the knowledge concerning all year-tourism, and the link between regional and mobile knowledge is very rich due to a strong knowledge interaction with other public tourism actors within and outside the region as a result of ToD collaboration with VisitDenmark and VisitNordjylland in the development of all-year tourism. The administrative core generally uses many different sources of knowledge with respect to the redevelopment phase, but mostly stem from the activities initiated by the regional and national tourism policy actors. The administrative core actors can be said to interpret mobile knowledge in the light of the destination's situation, but the extent to which ToD's administrative core, and thus ToD as a whole, obtain useful knowledge from the national and regional tourism actors is more debatable because the other destinations in both the national and regional projects are at very different stages of development and/or have very different tourism products. Instead, ToD is used as a case of good practice especially on the regional level, and by sharing ideas, knowledge and experiences, ToD helps to develop North Jutland's tourism sector with regard to, for instance, organizational structure and collaboration among the local tourism actors; thus, energizing tourism policy development elsewhere and placing the administrative core in a position where it also influences the knowledge processes outside the destination and, indeed, the region.

As summarized in Table 5, the analysis has shown that ToD's knowledge sources are many and that knowledge links and characteristics within ToD differ according to the identified actor groups, just as it varies according to which phase of tourism policy development is being analysed. But what is also evident is that ToD has generally played a very active role in transferring knowledge, originally primarily by anchoring external knowledges by adapting them to local needs, but recently in connection with the attempt to reposition itself as an all-year destination also by influencing knowledge processes outside the destination by sharing the organizational and other experiences with the tourism actors in other parts of Denmark.

5. Conclusion and Perspectives

The analysis has documented that ToD in the emergence phase primarily focused on developing joint-marketing activities and its overall organizational set-up, whereas the current redevelopment phase is focusing mainly on the product development through, for instance, new and innovative network and partnership activities with both the national and regional tourism actors as well as the non-traditional tourism actors within the destination. In terms of tourism policy change, this indicates a gradual move away from the fragmented, locally-based and on-site, service-oriented approach of the pre-ToD era, via joint accommodation services and marketing established in the emergence phase of the DMO, towards a more comprehensive strategy combining product development and promotion which resembles a rebranding strategy.

The analysis would seem to support the conclusion that the issue of localism has been effectively addressed by establishing and operating ToD as a network-based body where the individual stakeholders are mutually dependant on specific capacities of their partners, a consensual style of decision-making is prevailing, and a division of labour has been established that engages the local actors in the destination-wide tasks while at the same time enabling them to maintain close links with the tourism SMEs in their area. The weakening of localism is also demonstrated by the ready acceptance of the increased role of the administrative core in the early stage of the current redevelopment project, indicating a pragmatic attitude towards what otherwise could have been construed as undue centralization in the important agenda-setting stage of the policy process. This overcoming of the localist tendencies has undoubtedly been furthered by the patterns of knowledge interactions that have developed within ToD: very rich, internal-knowledge flows with an ongoing role for both the local level and the administrative core in generating different types of knowledge, a long tradition of contextualizing external knowledges, and an increasing impact on the policy processes outside the destination itself. Although the actors do not recall any knowledge gaps with regard to the emergence of ToD and generally are very satisfied with the present knowledge interactions, the interviewees still suggest that there is room for improvement, such as, internally, a greater involvement of the retail business throughout the destination as they contribute to the total tourism experience not least regarding the development of all-year tourism, and, involving greater distance, an enrichment of collaborative activities and concrete sharing of research findings concerning ToD and tourism in general, as the current relationship is characterized by ToD participating in interviews and contributing with various information but seldom getting feedback.

In both the emergence and the redevelopment of ToD, the internal wish for change has clearly been stimulated by extra-destinational incentives—EU funding for the original joint reservation system and VisitDenmark funding for the all-year tourism project—and this could of course suggest that lack of financial resources has hampered the development of ToD's strategies for destination development. After all, prolonging the tourism season and strengthening the destination through collaboration and knowledge sharing has been an issue of development since the mid-1990s, but while the external funding may have been an important facilitator, the question of timing would also seem to be of great importance. On the one hand, the perceived success of ToD as a joint venture has now made it easier to allocate resources to tourism development activities, on the other hand, only after the internal territorial cohesion of the DMO had been established would it have been feasible to proceed to addressing the new and potentially even bigger challenges of extensive product development and rebranding of the destination. Now, ToD as a network organization appears to be ready for this challenge, and the policies pursued with its emphasis on networking and learning are clearly moving closer to what is normally associated with the innovative product-development policies and hence, if successful, would take the destination in the direction of becoming a tourism cluster rather than just loosely joined co-located independent economic actors. But whether this will happen—and indeed whether destination TOD has made significant strides towards becoming an all-year tourism destination in 2015—also depend on other actors: while a well-functioning and well-communicating DMO will be important for such a venture, overcoming short-termism will also require that private providers of tourist services can be seriously committed to the project, and, of course, that ultimately the thought of North Jutland in October or March will appeal to a sufficient number of tourists. Successful organization of mutual network dependencies within the destination would seem to be a prerequisite for achieving policy change, but still developing new tourist experiences that will appeal to potential visitors will of course be the next and even more important challenge that must be addressed.

Acknowledgements

The research reported in this article was undertaken as part of the "EURODITE" Integrated Project sponsored by the EU's 6th Framework Programme (see www.eurodite.bham.ac.uk). While full responsibility for the paper remains with the authors, constructive comments from participants in the Regional Studies Association research network on "Tourism, Regional Development and Public Policy" in Izmir and Aalborg are gratefully acknowledged.

Note

1. Since the geographic area of the destination TOD and its DMO share the same name, the DMO will be referred to as ToD.

References

Ache, P. (2002) Cluster concepts – The social engineering of a new regional institutional fix, in: P. Raines (Ed.) *Cluster Development and Cluster Policy*, pp. 7–20 (Aldershot: Ashgate).

Arbejdsmarkedsstyrelsen (2008) *Beskæftigelsen i Nordjylland 2007. 7.000 flere job på et år.* København: Arbejdsmarkedsstyrelsen.

Bellini, N. & Pasquini, F. (1998) Towards a second generation regional development agency – The case of ERVET in emilia-romagna, in: H. Halkier (Ed.) *Regional Development Agencies in Europe*, pp. 253–270 (London: Jessica Kingsley).

Butzin, A., Helmstädter, E., Larsson, A., MacNeill, S., Vale, M. & Widmaier, B. (2007) *Guidelines to the WP6 Firm Level Case Studies* (Birmingham: EURODITE).

Cawley, M., Marsat, J.-B. & Gilmore, D. (2007) Promoting integrated rural tourism: Comparative perspectives on institutional networking in France and Ireland, *Tourism Geographies*, 9(4), pp. 405–420.

Cooke, P. (2001) Clusters as key determinants of economic growth: The example of biotechnology, in: Å. Mariussen (Ed.) *Cluster Policies – Cluster Development*, pp. 23–38 (Stockholm: Nordregio).

Cooke, P. & Morgan, K. (1998) *The Associational Economy* (Oxford: Oxford University Press).

Crevoisier, O., Helmstädter, E., Larsson, A., Widmaier, B., Vale, M. & Burfitt, A. (2007) *The Guidelines for the Empirical Research of the Work Packages 5 and 6* (Birmingham: EURODITE).

Dredge, D. (2006) Policy networks and the local organisation of tourism, *Tourism Management*, 27(2), pp. 269–280.

Fayos-Solá, E. (1996) Tourism policy: A midsummer night's dream? *Tourism Management*, 17(6), pp. 405–412.

Halkier, H. (2006) *Institutions, Discourse and Regional Development. The Scottish Development Agency and the Politics of Regional Policy* (Brussels: PIE Peter Lang).

Halkier, H. & Damborg, C. (1997) *Networks, Development Agencies and Intelligent Regions – Towards a Framework for Empirical Analysis*, European Studies Series of Occasional Papers 22, Aalborg: European Research Unit, Aalborg University.

Hall, C. M. (2008) *Tourism Planning: Policies, Processes and Relationships*, 2nd ed. (Harlow: Pearson Prentice-Hall).

Henriksen, P. F. (2008) *Knowledge Dynamics in the Making of the Top of Denmark Destination Management Organisation in North Jutland, Denmark*, TRUprogress 6, Aalborg: Aalborg University.

Hjalager, A.-M. (2000) Tourism destinations and the concept of industrial districts, *Tourism and Hospitality Research*, 2(3), pp. 199–213.

Hogwood, B. W. (1992) *Trends in British Public Policy. Do Governments Make any Difference?* (Buckingham: Open University Press).

Hogwood, B. W. & Gunn, L. A. (1986) *Policy Analysis for the Real World* (Oxford: Oxford University Press).

Hood, C. (1994) *Explaining Economic Policy Reversals* (Buckingham: Open University Press).

Jamal, T. B. & Getz, D. (1995) Collaboration theory and community tourism planning, *Annals of Tourism Research*, 22(1), pp. 186–204.

Kvistgaard, P. (2006) *Problemer og Magt i Regional Turismepolicy* (Aalborg: Aalborg Universitetsforlag).

Newlands, D. (2003) Competition and cooperation in industrial clusters; The implications for public policy, *European Planning Studies*, 11(5), pp. 521–532.

Rhodes, R. A. W. & Marsh, D. (1992) New directions in the study of policy networks, *European Journal of Political Research*, 21(1–2), pp. 181–195.

Saxena, G. (2005) Relationships, networks and the learning regions: Case evidence from the peak district national part, *Tourism Management*, 26(2), pp. 277–289.

Saxenian, A. (1985) Silicon valley and route 128: Regional prototypes or historic exceptions? in: M. Castells (Ed.) *High Technology, Space and Society*, pp. 81–105 (London: Sage).

Steiner, M. & Ploder, M. (2008) Structure and strategy within heterogeneity: Multiple dimensions of regional networking, *Regional Studies*, 42(6), pp. 793–816.

Thorelli, H. B. (1986) Networks: Between markets and hierarchies, *Strategic Management Journal*, 7(1), pp. 37–51.

Toppen af Danmark (2006) *Turismepolitik for Toppen af Danmark*, marts 2006, Frederikshavn: Toppen af Danmark.

Toppen af Danmark (2007a) *Pressemeddelelse*, January 2007, Frederikshavn: Toppen af Danmark.

Toppen af Danmark (2007b) *Ansøgning – Super-helårsdestination,* Frederikshavn: Toppen af Danmark.

Culinary Tourism as a Tool for Regional Re-equilibrium

ARMANDO MONTANARI & BARBARA STANISCIA

Dipartimento di Studi Europei e Interculturali, Sapienza Università di Roma, Piazzale Aldo Moro 5, 00185 Rome, Italy

ABSTRACT *This paper is the result of research undertaken into the relationship between quality agriculture and wine-and-food tourism on the Apennines of central and southern Italy. Food is not merely a source of nourishment: depending on production methods, food can also become a cultural reference point, an element of regional development and a tourist resource. This occurs with "local" food, representing a model of production and consumption which suggests a strong link with the region in which the food is produced. In the marginal mountainous regions of central Italy, there is an important productive segment involving motivated and innovative entrepreneurs, regardless of the public sector that is not always up to the situation. Tourism linked to quality agriculture has not only proved to be an economic lever but a form of protection of a territory that is fragile and at risk; it is a sort of contemporary sustainable development. The process is at the initial phases and in need of public support according to a bottom-up approach.*

1. Introduction

In the pages that follow, the results of research conducted during the last 3 years (2004–2007) are presented, and will show the relationship between quality agriculture and wine-and-food tourism on the Italian Apennines. This relationship, which in the past was either inexistent or conflicting, has proved to be worthy and able to trigger off endogenous development in marginal areas. It has also proved to be important in addressing the balance between developed areas (case study: coastal areas) and areas that are late in developing (case study: internal mountainous areas). This research is based on the results of an extensive fieldwork in the Apennines Region carried out from June 2004 to December 2005. A total of 34 in-depth semistructured interviews were conducted. Key persons were: 21 farmers active in the field of agritourism, and producing wine, cheese, olive oil, cereals and pulses, tomato sauce, jams, sausages, honey and pasta, and 13 entrepreneurs operating in the tourism field and representatives of local authorities. The interviews and the following focus group were finalized to identify strengths and weaknesses of the system, and the opportunities for consequent policies.

This article is structured as follows: in Section 2, there is a literature review relating to the topic and highlighting how the studies demonstrate recent attention given to the subject and its results that converge towards a global scale. In Section 3, the methodology that was followed during the research is illustrated, emphasizing the importance of qualitative analysis and of the use of subjective methods. In Section 4, the positive elements that are important to the connection between agriculture and wine-and-food products of quality-tourism in the area of the central-southern Apennines, are highlighted and evidence looked at concerning the pros and cons of territory and businesses. In Section 5, the territorial organization of the area is taken into account, as well as the importance of rural landscapes and quality food production and of the possibilities of re-balancing coasts with inland territories; there is a specific reference to a successful agricultural business that combines quality food products and tourism. Finally, the article ends with the conclusion.

The article contributes to the present debate on the relationships between quality food and tourism, giving a proper recognition to the role of landscape: the food of quality is part of the quality of its "terroir". Only under these conditions food is able to attract tourists and contribute to the regional economic re-equilibrium.

2. Background

Hall (2006) identifies culinary tourism with the one that is often defined as gastronomic or wine-and-food tourism and explains that it is a phenomenon that developed at the beginning of this decade. The adjective culinary that indicates everything connected with cooking and kitchen derives from the Latin "culina", meaning kitchen or cooking, that for metonymy also means meal, food and dish. Although the term has become synonymous of quality and good taste, unfortunately it derives from Latin as a deformation of "culus", bottom, that the etymologists Cortellazzo and Zolli (1999) justify because often lavatories were next to the kitchens. It is not surprising then that in recent years, there have been copious production of papers in scientific journals and even volumes published on this subject.

2.1 *Food and Tourism*

The relationship between food and tourism should be further investigated, how it has been interpreted by scholars and the general public, and we should try to understand why it has taken so long for this to happen. Cohen and Avieli (2004) provide us a key reading that was written to remind us that although food is considered as a tourist attraction, in reality the complications and the impediments are much greater. The same concept of tourism supposes that spending a period more or less short in an unknown environment can also be considered repulsive when the food is the product of culinary habits that are often not very well known. The presence of ethnic restaurants, in various cities of the world, does not seem to operate as a tool of cultural mediation as the authenticity of their supply is often debatable or approximate. That paper was born out of an international conference on "local food and tourism" that was held in Cyprus in the year 2000. It is reported that the same behaviour of the attendants confirmed the hypothesis that "local food" becomes largely acceptable only when it is totally or partially transformed. This is true especially for tourists from industrialized countries who visit places that are late in developing. Cohen and Avieli (2004) leave out the experiences of those tourists who travel to countries with a similar economic development to the one which they left behind.

2.2 *Agriculture and Tourism*

Telfer and Wall (1996) consider the relationship between agriculture and tourism through a wide review of the existing literature. The two sectors have been so far intensely competitive in the use of natural resources, such as soil and water, and in attracting economic resources. Belisle (1983) considers that food represents at least a third of tourist expenditures, but in regions and countries that have been late in developing their agricultural sector—due to physical, behavioural, economical, technological and marketing obstacles—there is a struggle to relate to quality, quantity and frequency of tourist demand and therefore there is often a request for imported products. However, Socher and Tschurtschenthaler (1994) maintain that agriculture can offer tourism not only alimentary but also intangible products such as the protection and creation of quality landscapes, where production costs hardly ever offer direct economical returns.

2.3 *Agriculture, Food and Tourism as Tools for Endogenous Development*

The picture of difficulties and reciprocal suspicions had started to dissolve when it became clear that these economic sectors, when operating in a synergic way, can favour and re-balance local development. Culinary tourism not only combines tourism with food. Food should be produced locally as much as possible in order to contribute to local development processes that are able to assert themselves against global competition. Hall (2006) affirms that the interest shown by tourists in the products, and therefore local culture, can contribute to stimulate the interest of local societies for this type of quality agricultural production. It is not only positive for the re-introduction and maintenance of genetic diversities but also for the reinforcement of community pride, and for the recovery of local identity and culture. Culinary tourism can develop both in urban and rural areas. Neal (2006) carried out a research in 243 cities of the US and four typologies emerged according to whether the food offered was primarily quantitative (culinary deserts) or presented a qualitative type of cultural dimension (gastronomic oases). Creative classes seek the characteristics of gastronomic oases according to the definition that Florida (2005) gives. While in urban areas the culinary offer merges with creative and innovative demand, in rural areas the most meaningful relationship is the one between food that should be produced locally and tourism, because this, as Hall (2006) maintains, represents a meaningful opportunity for local development.

2.4 *From Farm to Fork*

The "local food", that in some ways was lost as a product and as a culture, had been swept away by the undesirable effects of the globalization of food. It had to be researched, studied and brought back to light as a contributor to culture and above all, as a necessity to the health of people. A global farm agri-food product, for example, is a pot of yoghurt which—as per the principles of the rationality governing production adopted by the multinationals—has to travel a distance of at least 8000 km to reach the consumer, according to the results of a study carried out in Europe by Wuppertal Institute (Weizsäcker *et al.*, 1997). In the US, more than 60% of the population is classed as obese, or overweight, and approximately a third of the younger generation is following the same model. In the 2004 documentary film "Super Size Me", the director Morgan Spurlock exposes this situation, subjecting himself to an intensive course of breakfast, lunch and dinner from fast-food chains for a month, rapidly ending up putting his own health at risk. In 2004, the University of Iowa's Leopold Centre for Sustainable Agriculture initiated a study on "A geography of taste: Iowa's potential for developing place-based and traditional foods". Pirog and Paskiet (2004) start from the fact that there exists a niche in the market in which the producers deal with the consumers directly, offering products that are highly distinctive, rather than the standardized and repetitive ones. The excesses of globalization and its negative consequences to human health, generated by foods produced with methods of advanced industrialization, have certainly contributed to the re-territorialization of food. Additionally, in the US—where the large chains of fast food used to boast of serving millions of meals a day for a long time—a tendency towards a healthy life has been developing and has contributed to forming a new food culture, although it is still for a minority. Shortridge and Shortridge (1998) began to utilize, during the 1990s, the concept of "geography of taste" intended as an expression and identification of regional and ethnic food.

2.5 *Local Food: A Tentative Definition*

The expression "regional food", or even "ethnic food", creates confusion among the consumers and leaves broad spaces to "purposeful" inaccuracies in communication and attempts at fraud. Rightly Hall *et al.* (2003) have highlighted that consumers do not differentiate between products defined as "locally produced" and "local specialities" while what is relevant instead is precisely the difference that such confusion creates in terms of politics of local development. Nummendal and Hall (2006) propose to use the definition suggested by the report of Enteleca Research and Consultancy (2000). In this report, not only is food produced locally considered to be "local food" but also the dishes that do not require imported raw materials and that then assume a regional or local identity because they are processed in the area. The meaning of "local food" as it is referred to here seems too limited to the physical place. The explanation offered by Bessière (1998) includes symbolic virtues to food and a sense of community, an indicator of belonging to a social group, of a state of mind, symbol, dream, an element to remember. Feagan (2007), making reference to the supply chain of food in global production indicates the reduction in size of the supply chain—therefore the consumer is getting closer to the producer and to the place of origin of the food—as a way to re-establish the capacity of the regions to produce profits. The concepts of "terroir" and "denomination of origin" add a positive grouping between food and geography to the supply chain. Montanari *et al.* (2008) also focus on the concept of the supply chain of wine-and-food quality products. The supply chain can, in fact, be the tool used to reduce the distance between the consumer, places of production and the various local actors who intervene in the production. In industrial production, the consumer is unaware of the place where the food is produced and who produces it—and it could not be otherwise—since the place has a vast dimension—that tends to coincide with the world—and the producer coincides with an administrative counsel, which represents a vague number of shareholders. In these forms of industrial production, the consumer does not identify the producer, and not even the place of production, since in the best of cases he sees them, or he imagines them, through a message of a TV commercial, and therefore as "non-places", in the meaning that Augé (1995) gives to it.

2.6 *Culinary Tourism as Tool of Endogenous Development: Evidences from Germany, Spain and US*

These reflections have been confirmed by empirical studies conducted in various industrialized countries, where the problem of the areas that are late in developing is not generalized but confined to limited regions and for reasons that are not easily identifiable. Job and Murphy (2006) have examined the relationship between wine production, wine tourism and endogenous regional development in the Valley of the Mosel in Germany. This type of development has become necessary due to the risk of decline that may have affected wine production, caused by territories that are very steep, creating operative difficulties and high management costs. An agency for regional development has been created with the specific aim of coordinating marketing activities and ensuring maximum synergy between the production of wine and the tourist sector. It has permitted maintaining a consistent flow of wine tourists who have provided a contribution to the production of wine and therefore to maintaining the wine-landscape. Armesto López and Gómez Martín (2006) refer to the case of the Catalan province of Priorat (Spain) in which the valorization of gastronomic resources has permitted both the development of tourism as well as the promotion and commercialization of quality agricultural products. Priorat is an area that is late in developing within one of the most industrialized and developed regions of Spain. The increase of the tourist flows and the economic and social opportunities that have followed have constituted the necessary base for endogenous development. Che (2006) reflects on the role of farm-holidays in Michigan, US, in relation to similar experiences that accrued in Europe. Within the sphere of the marketing programme "Select Michigan", Che (2006) points out a few problems that could significantly affect the success of this type of development strategy. The author brings to light the need to point out the specificity of local products, proximity to the large urban centres that facilitate the access of tourists and visitors, the growing willingness of the consumers to pay more for quality products that are healthier and the reduced impact on the environment when producing them. This research also points out that tourism based on quality agriculture, as well as re-launching the production of food, constitutes a barrier against the abandonment of the territory; therefore it has a positive effect on the politics of land use even in metropolitan areas—checks of the sprawl phenomena—and, therefore, in the whole State.

3. Methodology

The methodology of research has been adapted to the characteristics of the analysed phenomenon. As it is dealing with a phenomenon with a qualitative content, which is characterized by the softness of the content, "soft" methods of qualitative analysis have been chosen: (i) environmental scanning, (ii) interviews with key informants and (iii) a focus group.

The use of qualitative analyses has been discussed for a long time even in the literature about tourism. Walle (1997) faces the comparison between quantitative and qualitative research. Part of the task—that he does not agree with, but that prevails in the current debate—is that quantitative research is considered to be scientific, while qualitative research is considered to be artistic. The former, therefore, is seen to be rigorous and reliable, while the latter is not. The author examines the consideration of the two methods from an anthropological point of view that, exceeding the scientific/artistic dichotomy, reaches the more sophisticated one of etic/emic to define the two types of research. He underlines how anthropology uses them both to study the different phenomena and reaches the conclusion that a similar approach should be used for the studies on tourism. The author proposes to use quantitative research when there are adequate data and time available to analyse them; when, however, the phenomena are such that they cannot be put into a model using data and time available is limited, he proposes to use qualitative research. The reflection is that often, the use of the so-called scientific rigour results in trivial and obvious conclusions—despite having been rigorously demonstrated—while the use of qualitative methods may result in conclusions that—despite not having been rigorously proved—could reveal themselves to be enlightening, as the results of science should be. Tribe (1997) argues whether tourism is a discipline or not and concludes that it is not. In doing so, he confronts the issues of whether tourism is a science or not. With this purpose, he asserts that tourism is not a science and that scientific methods (i.e. quantitative) are not the only suitable methods to study this sector. In fact "in proposing scientific method as the method of tourism analysis, one would necessarily exclude large parts of the phenomenal world of tourism which are not scientifically quantifiable and are not indeed scientific puzzles" (Tribe, 1997, p. 646).

(i)   Taking a hint from the methodology that Gordon and Glenn (1999) define as "environmental scanning", used for forecasting and scenario building, a preliminary analysis of the spatial context and sector of study has been carried out. An appeal was made to examine specific literature—local, national and international—to analyse available quantitative data, to research on websites. This first phase of research, which is explorative, has served to identify the subjects and criticalities that would need to be faced in the following phases.

(ii) The method of interviewing key informants has been used for a long time in empirical investigations (see, for example, Tremblay, 1982) and even, more recently, in research that involve the tourist sector and the one involving local food (Webb et al., 1998; Fawcett & Cormack, 2001; Telfer, 2001; Fallon & Kriwoken, 2003). It is a subjective method that provides information of a qualitative nature (Pacinelli, 2008). The key informants are people who for their history, knowledge and inclusion within the community in question are able to provide valid and credible information on phenomena on which they are informed. In the literature (Fabbris, 1991), three types of key informants can be identified: anthropological and/or cultural informants, representatives and/or informants of the community and the experts. Each of them has knowledge and different information available with respect to time: the first inform primarily on the past of the community in question, the second inform on the present and the third can help to predict future tendencies. In the research of which the results are presented here, 34 people have been interviewed belonging to the three above-mentioned groups. They are entrepreneurs who produce quality wine–food products, entrepreneurs who commercialize them, restaurant owners, eco farm-holiday entrepreneurs, representatives of associations of agriculture and tourist enterprises, representatives of public bodies and representatives of cultural associations such as Slow Food. They have been selected with the snowballing method, starting from those who are well known in the field and through them, arriving at those who are less well known but still informed on the facts. Their opinions have been recorded using face-to-face in-depth semi-structured interview; this type of interviews has been preferred to questionnaires which may have presented some rigidity. The community in question that does not have distinct socio-territorial characteristics is represented by 34 chosen people. It is characterized by the ideal and virtual adhesion to four necessary ideas: (i) quality production, (ii) production tied to territory and history, (iii) production as a cultural vehicle and (iv) a supply chain that is short and closed. The whole is completed and complemented by tourist experience for the consumer/beneficiary.

(iii) From the interviews of key informants, a few key ideas have emerged into which it was thought appropriate to look at depth through a focus group in which 15 of the 34 key informants were involved and interviewed (Montanari *et al.*, 2008). The focus groups (Glenn, 1999) are closed meetings, not open to the public, and only available by direct invitation by the organizers. They are used to focus the attention of the participants on one or a limited number of subjects, to discuss and to reach operative proposals. The people who are invited are persons chosen for their competences in the sector and on the subject. The invitations have to be formal and expressed through a letter accompanied by a description of what will happen and points to be discussed. The meeting takes place around a round table, in which all the participants have the same importance, and hierarchical levels do not exist. Everyone is invited to express themselves freely and to confront the subject starting from their own ideas and experiences, avoiding considerations of a general character that do not have any explicative value. The facilitator—the person who conducts the focus group—has in mind or in front of him/her, a scheme to follow that must not be rigid. The scheme should be a guide for the discussion but not a constraint to it. New ideas that guide the researchers emerge from the discussion that, generally, does not last more than 2 h. In the focus group conducted for the research presented here, the central theme has been the constitution of an agency of endogenous development that would promote the territory through the support of the agricultural and tourist enterprises that offer quality wine–food products.

4. A Network for Endogenous Development

The themes discussed with the key informants and later deepened by the focus group referred to the actual situation and future scenarios.

The actual situation was the subject of analysis and valuation. The phase of analysis predicted reflections on: (i) the wine–food products susceptible to tourist attraction, (ii) the way in which the richness of wine–food products has been passed on in time, (iii) the supply chains and (iv) the relationship between local quality products and the offer of cultural assets. In this phase, every single producer has become aware of the presence of other wine–food products within the same territory. Culinary products have undergone a process of rarefaction owing to different phenomena of the last century that have had severe consequences on the productive cycles. Examples of these are emigrations that emptied the countryside, recurring economic crises that have deprived the sector of the necessary economic resources and innovative processes, phenomena of intensification and mechanization of agriculture that have forced farmers to choose more productive species to the detriment of quality. The quality product has been re-discovered only in recent years, a few decades ago at the most. It has never been a continual process trans-mitted from generation to generation. The producers of today who operate with innovation and success are hardly ever the children of the producers of yesterday. Sometimes they can be their grandchildren or great-grandchildren; therefore, there has been a generational leap, so who then, has contributed more greatly to maintaining traditions? Have the tra-ditions been effectively preserved? Camillo, an incoming tour operator, who was born and operates in Abruzzo but has studied in Florence says:

> ...I would make a distinction between grandparents, parents and children. Tra-ditional food has represented for grandparents and, as a reflection, but to a lesser extent, to the parents a symbol of indigence, impoverishment and a social marginal situation that would have taken place in the years before the war or immediately afterwards. These foods have been abandoned and their traditions with them. The process of negation of the past has reached the point of selling furniture, kitchen cup-boards and old chests for very little money in order to buy furniture made out of chip wood. The same has happened with the typical local handicraft and wine–food pro-ducts. The children, however, are rediscovering these traditions. I do not know how much we can speak of continuity; of course, someone stayed behind to grow runner beans but in a marginal way, in extremely remote areas, where it was not done because it represented a continuity of the family tradition, it was done because there were no alternative ways of social and economic development. Therefore, in the towns high up, surrounded by castle walls on the top of hills, the small family plot was still used for these productions. Perhaps the grandfather had stayed behind to cultivate the land, the son had moved to the city and forgotten everything, the grandchild, however, had studied, gained a culture and then went to search for his traditions and found his grandfather who still had his little plot of runner beans and the tradition was then re-valued.

Other producers, however, recognize how important the role of continuity is in the transfer of wine–food traditions in a family line; a role that they think was expressed in various ways. It is a diversified tradition that has been expressed in families in relation to their social standing and economic capacity; there were traditions of "poor food" and traditions of "rich food". Today the richness is in the tradition—not in the food itself—that contem-plates an asset that is certainly more costly than similar industrial products and that con-siders both the basic raw materials and the value-added bestowed by labour, inventiveness, creativity and all of the connected services that are offered. Historically, at the moment in which the product that we define today as a quality product was abandoned inappropri-ately, following market demand, it started following a double road: quantity was needed to earn money and to get by, while the quality product was needed to survive and was for the use of the whole family. In recent years, in many cases, the production of quantity has been abandoned as it was no longer rewarding and the production of quality increased, but in reality, it had never been abandoned. The family has, in addition, served as a cultural incubator; for example, a well-known producer of cereals in the regional territory has certainly benefited from the fact that her grandfather had continued for years to cultivate a small piece of land with spelt. An ulterior theme has been the one about supply chains. The producer of quality products knows exactly what they are and how they work but often does not know how to improve them. The quality wine–food product should be considered the same as a cultural asset, indeed, it is a cultural asset, and it can take advantage of the reciprocal synergies as the assets have a greater rooting in the conscience of society. The sheep is the emblematic product of the Apennines since it is the element of connection between the wine–food product and the territory. The sheep, queen of the mountain and transhumance, sinks its roots into the culture of both the ancient and contemporary territories. Notwithstanding this fact, it has been a few decades since sheep breeding has had its funds withdrawn by the public sector. Nunzio, breeder and producer of sheep's cheese thinks that

> . . .a certain interpretation in a modernist key wanted to relegate the role of the sheep to a symptom of underdevelopment. The politicians in their electoral meetings used to say, "You should thank us because we have transformed you as you used to be a nation of shepherds", conferring to the sector a negative meaning. Some time later I replied to one of them, "Now we are a nation of redundant workers, we are a nation of postal workers in early retirement and surely with a future a lot less rosy than the one that the shepherds could look forward to" (. . .) and these unfortunately are political choices that are influenced by backward considerations (. . .) that consider pasturing as a disvalue. Our initiative, however, has had the merit of re-proposing the image of the sheep with new values, that have above all an environmental character, because a sheep does so much more for example, than a forest ranger or any other guardian in the defence from fires. . .

The relationship between culinary products and cultural assets is essential for the development of tourism. The Abbey of San Giovanni in Venere (eleventh to thirteenth century), in Fossacesia, a little town in Central Italy, dominates the plain and sea from a hill covered in olive trees. The olive-grove, which belongs to the monks, has been entrusted for its production to Giuseppe, who produces olive oil of a very high quality and who looks after a vegetable cultural asset as he recounts,

> ..the tree that is right under the Abbey of San Giovanni in Venere is nearly 1,000 years old, maybe even older, but it is the oldest olive tree in Abruzzo. This plant has been abandoned for many years, me and a group of technicians rescued it, obviously I live in Fossacesia, I went to school nearby the Abbey, I very nearly became a monk and therefore have a special relationship with this area. I longed to bring back to life the plant that was sitting there dying and abandoned. We carried out this operation and maybe even went further in exceeding the rosier of expectations. The plant today is the most visited place in Fossacesia area. . .

The discussion of the usability of cultural assets should not, however, only be made for tourists; it should also be made in relation to residents. Cultural assets exist, but often are not at all perceived by residents, or at best, are perceived in an insufficient way.

Hospitality presupposes that the guest should know from the beginning what he can and cannot do. Many important cultural assets are not very well perceived by residents because they are not fully visible in the contemporary conscience of the places and, therefore, are difficult to access and visit. The tourist learns of those assets from the guides but then cannot visit them because they are not regularly open to the public and nobody knows precisely when they are open, or are inaccessible.

During the phase of the research dedicated to the valuation, the main themes have been those of the certification of quality and perceived importance by the producers. At the international level, the situations in the US and EU are compared. The first is based on the prevalence of industrialization and globalization; it focuses its attention on the concept of trademark on the company's brand. According to this concept, the product of a reliable company should be indifferent to the place of production: to the consumer what matters is the guarantee given by the brand. EU policies, however, have encouraged an involvement with the territory based on strengthening capabilities and potentials, even commercial ones, and all the denominations of origin. The mark of quality has appeared in this context and failed for its inability to present itself in an unambiguous manner: it does not show a typical regional product to set against the denominations of origin nor a commercial brand above the territorial context.

These differences in approach are particularly important to those companies that export to the American market, as it demands continuous analysis, research and certificates. The processes were unfamiliar to most of the enterprises and in some cases those who sent out goods to that market did not value them.

Generally, the certifications of quality are a positive matter for companies that are organized in an industrial manner and in a market that is either national or international. The certification, however, adds little value to agricultural quality production related to the territory and its culture and traditions. If the territory must be "brought" to the consumer, the certifications are a necessary form of protection. However, if the consumer has to be "taken" to the territory to taste and buy its products, it does not make sense to use an international certification process in character and value, which is unfocused on the territory. In the first instance, the more a product is standardized, the more it benefits the product. This does not mean that certifications should not exist: it is clear, however, that for some regional quality products (for example, the saffron of Navelli or lentils of Santo Stefano di Sessanio, on the Apennines) the certification process does not add anything and does not take anything away from the quality of the product. The certifications, in fact, refer to the processes and not to the products.

Other reflections in the valuation phase have been directed to the relationship between producers and public administrations—the municipality, region, state and European Union—and the intermediary institutions. The small and medium enterprises commercialize their own production of quality, especially in the national retail sector, where communication is very personalized and "humane". There are no advertising campaigns, as with large companies, and communication is effected through a net of sales made by around 10 agents, and meetings are arranged with restaurant owners and retailers. Fairs are used as a meeting and gathering place. The mailing of trial samples is necessary to maintain the promotion of new products on a concrete base. Sometimes they also sponsor activities, displays and events that should be for the most part leading back to the ethos of the company. The public body—which represents the institutional aspect—should be with the private company, which represents the operative aspect that leads and promotes the product as part of the richness of the region. To collaborate means deciding together the best strategy, as the private company works constantly on the market and recognizes its needs and facets. Of course, the institution can undertake a promotional activity, perhaps by consulting a valued marketing agency; however, the approval of those who actually do the job can add knowledge, professionalism and methodology to the project. Wine and oil have both been considered among the tools of promotion.

In scenarios for the future, the opportunity to constitute an agency for territorial development has been valued based on a network set up by operators of the sector under consideration. Current thinking is that such an agency should be constituted with public–private investments, but should have a wholly private management. This is because the public sector is considered not to have the instruments to comprehend totally the needs of the enterprises and to fix effective objectives for them. Three main elements have been pushed to the forefront while facing the problem of the creation of the network and consequently of the agency.

  (i) The consumers of quality wine–food products, as is the case with culinary tourists, are people with a medium-high cultural level who have a good spending capacity. They make scrupulous choices and live and consume in relation to their choices. In order to satisfy this type of request, there is a need for people who know well the territory such as its geography, botany, history of art, culture and history and how to offer their knowledge to that type of demand that is prepared to spend but is also particularly demanding. The agency, therefore, should encourage the entrepreneurs to let their unexpressed knowledge rise to the surface and to form new recruits. It should lead research and development activities that the entrepreneurs, who are generally medium-small and have low sums of money available, and cannot implement on their own.
 (ii) In order to promote any new product, based on tradition, it is necessary to introduce in the field a particular entrepreneurial capacity. To reinforce such a spirit, the agency should create a network of knowledge and cultural references that is larger than the one a single company is able to introduce. It should create an enterprise culture through meetings, seminars and debates.
(iii) The level of satisfaction expressed by entrepreneurs towards public entities is not high. They state that the public and private sectors move at different speeds. The public tends to have general competencies that do not find a point of reference in the particular necessities of the productive sector. The agency should contribute by identifying the right channels for the promotion and diffusion of the products.

5. Food and Tourism, a Tool of Endogenous Development in the Mountain Areas Between the Adriatic and the Tyrrhenian Sea, Central Italy

The area of reference extends between the Tyrrhenian Sea, at the latitude of Rome, and the Adriatic Sea, at the latitude of Chieti-Pescara urban area, and includes the regions of Lazio and Abruzzo. It is an area that at the end of the Roman Empire (fourth century A.D.), and until the Unification of Italy (nineteenth century A.D.), remained fragmented and without internal connections due to the presence of the Apennine, that in this area reaches a little more than 2900 m (Mount Gran Sasso) and a little less than 2800 m (Mount Maiella). The distance between the two coasts, in relation to urban centres, is around 180 km and the principal mountain peaks are between 40 and 50 km from the Adriatic coast. The internal part of the mountain and hilly areas and hilly areas are more difficult to access and cover a strip that varies between 50 and 100 km, with a centre of gravity strongly shifted towards the Adriatic coast.

5.1 *Winescapes and Foodscapes Over Space*

In the area under consideration, the following typologies of landscape can be identified:

(1) Type 1: The mountains. The strip that includes the principal mountain areas with peaks exceeding 2000 m. In recent decades, it has endured processes of abandonment and social economic decline.
(2) Type 2: The hills. Sheltered by mountains, at the altitude of the hills, agriculture and rearing of livestock, apart from a few significant exceptions, have managed to survive more because of the obstinacy of human beings rather than acceptable socio-economic conditions.
(3) Type 3: Coastal plains. The strip of a few kilometres that includes the coastline, on which productive and settlement activities are concentrated as well as leisure and tourism. Conflicts concerning the use of the territory have developed over the use of water resources, atmospheric pollution, refuse and environment management.
(4) Type 4: Open sea. The strip next to the coast where coastal fishing activities are concentrated and seaside resorts and small coasting. This territory has been utilized too intensively, which has compromised its natural balance, and suffers from having had a too intensive use of its resources and from the introduction of pollutants.
(5) Type 5: High seas. The rest of the sea up to the limit of territorial waters. A marine area that has been subject for a long time to non-programmed forms of fishing that create grave imbalances of the reproductive capacities of resources.

5.2 *Winescapes and Foodscapes Over Time*

These typologies repeat themselves in an asymmetric way, although in different ways and differently, towards the Tyrrhenian and Adriatic Sea. The area under examination can be considered broadly during three historical periods, from an environmental point of view. In this case, reference is made to the side of the Apennine that descends towards the Adriatic. Until the first phase of industrialization (Figure 1) the main economic activities were agriculture and pasture, and the populations living in the hills managed forest and pasture areas. Some plains were utilized, some only received little use; on a few of these, winter pasturing was possible and, therefore, the main movements took place in a perpendicular direction towards the sea, in other cases the abandonment had favoured the expansion of swamps especially along rivers and streams. In Figure 1 the bottom of the Adriatic is characterized by emissions of methane gas coming from under the seabed that manifest as small muddy volcanoes.

Starting from the first phase of industrialization (Figure 2), the great North–South infrastructures have been built along the Adriatic coast, the railway in the nineteenth century and the motorway in the 1970s, productive settlements have been created along the principal axe of communication, and reclaimed plains have been urbanized and intensively anthropized. Over time, the coastline has been burdened with infrastructures connected

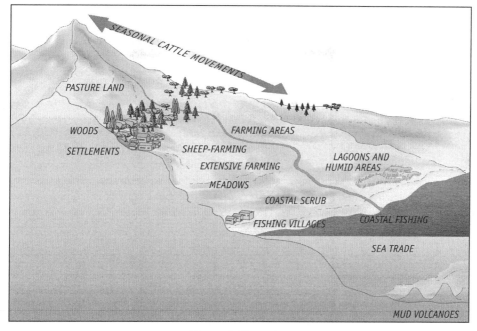

Figure 1. Yesterday

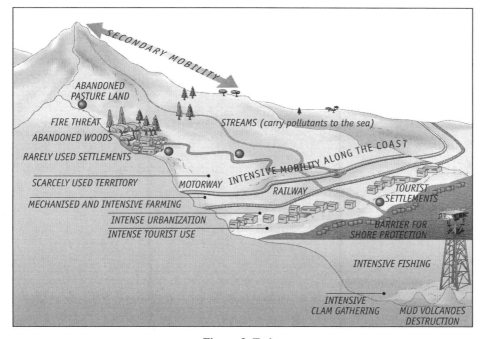

Figure 2. Today

with tourist and leisure activities, and efforts have tried to make it irremovable to defend its economic activities or the infrastructures and services that have been put into place in its proximity. Fishing activities have intensified lately, along the coast over-fishing has reduced numbers of different species of fish and intensive fishing has expanded into deeper waters. Today, we are going through a transition phase, mountain areas stood partly abandoned for many years and have therefore preserved their biological diversity and have become protected areas. Agriculture close to these areas discovers in biological re-conversion, its own productive and commercial convenience, the plain areas try to redeem themselves from a too-intensive use and the risk of compromising their own development, while coastal areas that are too anthropized are safeguarded. In Figure 3, a territorial system is described, based on sustainable development and environmental quality in which the protected areas are no longer casual phenomena determined by the reduced anthropization but a system of differentiated methods of environmental protection that finds its place of continuity on the coastline. To limit the protection of a certain

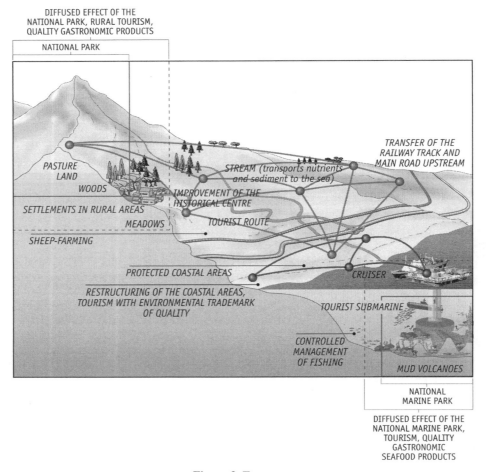

Figure 3. Tomorrow

number of areas would be very reductive and even counterproductive: the defence system, in fact, finds its more complete accomplishment only within a sustainable development process in which policies are put into practice to reach economic efficiency and social equity at the same time. The platforms for gas extraction, having ceased their extractive activity, may become artificial barriers in the creation of protective marine areas, as well as cornerstones for the realization of a system of artificial islands, where activities such as ecotourism, sport, recreation, scientific research and breeding of quality fish and molluscs take place. For a better connection to the territory, the productive supply chains have been shown, each one constituting a network of functions that is established on the territory and constitutes an element of connection with the other supply chains and with those of other products. In other parts of the territory, the supply chain of the production of sheep's milk and cheese are placed, followed lower down by the supply chain of cow's milk and dairy products. At the same altitude, locally grown cereals, bread and confectionary, together with olives and oil and wine supply chains can be found. The latter covers the lower hilly territories towards the sea where the breeding of fish and molluscs supply chains are placed.

5.3 *Territorial Typologies and Tourist Uses*

Seaside tourism, known for its long tradition, is the only industry in Italy that greatly lends itself to considerations facing the phases of evolution of supply and demand. It is undergoing an evolution that seems to have exhausted the trend of quantitative growth of the previous decades and depends for its further development on the introduction of parameters of quality connected to the concept of sustainability. The transformation of the coastal areas in the last few decades has followed a model of "tourist coastal areas" that recalls a Fordist type of tourism. In the early 1990s, it was felt that there was a need to re-organize the structure of coastal tourist settlements and to adjust the supply to the changed requirements of Italian consumers, but above all, to European consumers. Economic disposability of European society—limited by strict taxation policies that have also contributed to the increase of unemployment rates—have shaped the customer into being more careful about prices and meticulous in selecting and comparing the relationship between costs and benefits of the various offers that are on display. Furthermore, tourists from EU countries, that are so numerous in Italian coastal areas, have brought with them a great preoccupation with environmental quality, the measure of which is more evident and comparable today, thanks to the application of European directives. Since the measurement of environmental quality is particularly complex and has not yet found a common European denominator, the more relevant parameters considered today are: quality of air and management of atmospheric pollution in relation to mobility, quality of drinking and bathing water, management of water resources, recycling of refuse, defence and protection of the landscape.

Within the political sphere of re-positioning, the relevant coastal tourist product is the attempt at integration with internal areas to enrich what is on offer with components of natural and cultural heritage at a relatively modest distance from the coast thanks to: (a) a reduced consumption of the soil, (b) reinforcement of service activities, (c) reduced expansion of the new constructions in relation to the possibilities of reusing the existing buildings, (d) the slowing down or inversion of the migratory flows, (e) environmental conflicts referable to fragile resources and, therefore, now scarce, (f) carrying capacity and (g) environmental compatibility. This is above all, necessary in areas that are relatively vast that contain or are adjacent to human settlements, as is the case with protected areas not far from coastal areas.

The tourist product of the coastal areas should be developed based on the interrelationships among a vast range of resources—such as the sea, beach, accommodation and services—but also environmental qualities, cultural assets, gastronomy, artisanship and sport. In order to fully identify the phases of development of the coastal areas, the models of growth have been determined along with districts where the tourist phenomenon has developed in an integrated way. So far, the attempts to identify these districts have not had great success because the point of reference has been the concept of industrial district. The latter has the advantage of having been vastly studied both from a methodological and an empirical point of view but does not adapt very well to the peculiarity of the tourist sector that can, in summary, return to the following two aspects: the simultaneous nature of production and consumption and the coincidence between place of production and place of consumption. Other peculiarities of the tourist development areas can be traced back to geographical and temporal coincidences, such as the accentuated roles of the extra-economic networks, organizing and partnering, peculiarity of the horizontal economic networks, complexities of the decisional networks in the role of a subsidiary character and finally, the extraterritoriality of many economic actors, the most important being the Tour Operators.

Rural or natural tourism in inner areas cannot constitute an alternative to the tourist dynamics of the coast. For the intrinsic characteristics of this kind of tourism—the potential number of existing beds, feasible or retrievable, and their concentration in space, are not comparable with the one on the coast. It follows that tourism in inner areas constitutes a form of complementary tourism, which is useful especially to improve the dynamics of natural and cultural heritage without substituting the conventional coastal model as a strategic sector of regional economics. The integration between two complementary realities can serve to exalt the peculiar potentiality of tourism and re-establish a balance in the development process.

5.4 *Sheep's Milk and Cheese Supply Chain*

The farm/company of La Porta dei Parchi is located nearby the town of Anversa degli Abruzzi, at an altitude of 556 m, not far from the station of Cocullo of the A25 motorway that goes from Rome to Pescara, at the turning to Gole del Sagittario that is famous for its beauty. Landed property in the area is fragmented, intense division into plots accompany vast areas of public property, woodland and pastureland that belong to or are on the border with Parco Nazionale d'Abruzzo, Lazio and Molise. Stock-rearing that has been at the basis of mountain economy in these areas is now going through a period of crisis because of the serious depopulation of the area, the subsequent reduction of the number of heads, lack of manpower, high costs of production and scarce profits. The practice of winter transhumance towards pastureland of the plains of Tavoliere delle Puglie and Agro Romano is no longer possible and sheep breeding has become non-migratory, with vertical movements towards high pastures in the summer season. With only the production of wool, meat, milk and cheeses, the farm would not survive since high production costs are not recognized by the market where meat and wool have to endure competition from the world market, and cheeses cannot be competitive with products that are more famous.

The broad pasture containing a few herbs that appear on the surface, tiny streams interrupted here and there by stony covers of rubble is certainly suitable for sheep breeding. Meat, milk and cheese that are obtained are of high quality, but the costs of production are very high, local work force to take care of sheep is hard to find and the "new" shepherds are from Rumania and the inner areas of the Balkan Peninsula (Staniscia, 2003). In order to solve this situation, the company has individuated a number of side activities among which the most well known is "adopt a sheep", that ensures that the adopters are sent food products from the farm. This initiative has received much success at an international level with about a thousand articles in main daily international newspapers, television programmes on it in major industrialized countries and much attention received even from international researchers (Holloway *et al.*, 2006).

5.5 *Geography of Taste: Sheep Breeding*

Within the sphere of research, collaboration with the company has been established to identify and build a supply chain of sheep breeding that would identify the activities carried out and transform them, however necessary, to support tourist activities. This supply chain appears to be very short since the consumer is directly in contact with the producer and with the places of production; it identifies the activities in relation to the places in which these are carried out. As a result, it is possible to define a "geography of taste" of sheep breeding (Figure 4). The producer has chosen the sheep species in relation to the environment, landscape and environmental resources and, therefore, has re-introduced a traditional species to those places. It was an important decision to take since in a previous phase the race of sheep had been chosen for the quantity of the production in the attempt to compete on a global level, but its results were in vain. The producer programmed four productive lines: wool, cheese, meat and energy. The wool produced is not sold as a raw material, as this would not be remunerative, but is elaborated in the farm, thereby enhancing the phases of shearing, washing and removal of grease, dyeing with natural products and spinning. Each of these activities is carried out in a particular place and becomes the occasion for a tourist event. Cheese is made with sheep's milk: in winter it happens in the barn and in summer, after having done the vertical transhumance, it happens on the mountains. A small mobile cheese factory close to the pasture is used in the summer. The cheese is then refined and matured in special spaces close to the barns. In order to better commercialize meat, as well as sell it fresh, it is elaborated into packs for a better preservation. There is also an eco-holiday-farm and in the nearby village lodgings are offered in bed-and-breakfasts. What is produced is, therefore, served to the guests of the eco-holiday-farm and the bed-and-breakfasts. It is sold to the visitors and tourists and sent to the "sheep adopters" and, since the products are of high quality—a quality which is recognized for the prizes won in Italy and abroad—they are sold through specialized shops in some Italian and European cities. The farm has become specialized in the production of energy using water at the bottom of the valley, wind on top of the mountain, solar thermal and solar photovoltaic on the roofs of buildings, and biochemical using the excrements of the barn. The farm is, therefore, self-sufficient in energy consumption; it confirms its attention to the environment and its cautiousness, which is demonstrated by the organic breeding that it does. All the production processes have a didactic dimension in an area for school visits.

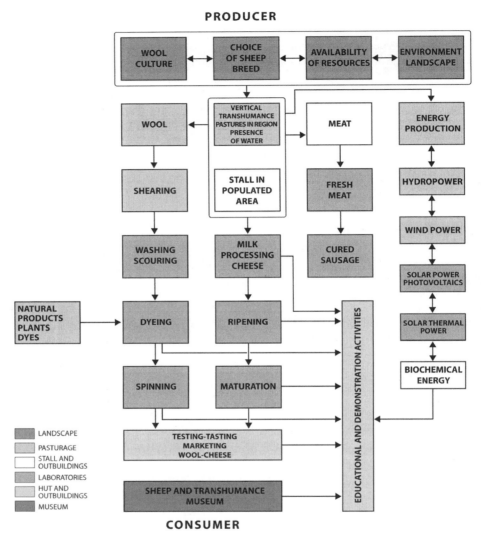

Figure 4. Sheep-farming, the geography of taste

5.6 *The Taste of Geography: Sheep Breeding*

Once the relationship between places and phases of the food cycle has been set up, they then moved on to programme a series of thematic routes to offer to visitors and tourists. From a food cycle that expresses itself through geography, it has moved onto places that find their justification through the interpretation of the food cycle: the taste of geography has confronted a taste of geography of sheep breeding. In Figure 5, the most meaningful points of the food cycle have been put on a map and some possible tourist itineraries have been indicated. The fundamental choices of the breeder are explained in the points that follow: (1) when a flock of sheep is placed against the beauty of the Gole del Sagittario and the richness of the protected areas. The Parco Nazionale is there

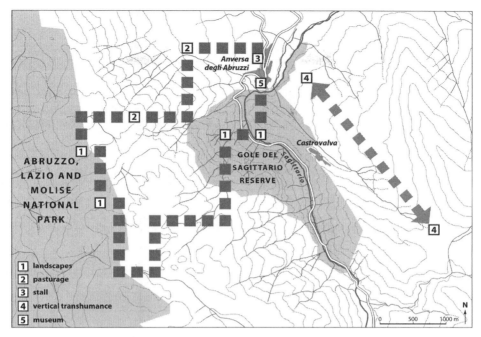

Figure 5. Sheep-farming, the taste of geography

for its biological diversities, it is the richness and herbs of the pastures that feed the sheep (2), and with the preoccupying presence of wolves that are always ready to attempt the integrity of the flock. It is also possible to visit the implants for the production of hydroelectric and wind energy. In point (3), the centre of the farm is shown where barns, eco-holiday-farm, educational spaces, cheese factory and implants for the production of solar and biochemical energy are placed. Along the route of transhumance (4), a tourist programme is developing for those who would like to experiment for a few days with the life of shepherds, sleeping and eating outside, milking the sheep and making cheese. Old buildings can be visited, reliving the exploits of the brigands of the nineteenth century; listening to old stories of bandits and sharing ancient poems and traditional music. Finally in point (5), near the urban centres, where the instruments of material culture are gathered and preserved, it is possible to go and discover or read about local culture in which sheep breeding was a fundamental part. These last products have received considerable success, especially abroad and been the object of articles in the international press, because they were considered to be innovative. The farm has not only reached its economic objectives but has favoured other similar farms present in the area, which have been awakened by a healthy spirit of emulation. A complex tourist offer has formed and evolved that will certainly give fruits in the near future.

6. Conclusion

The research has shed light on how in the area in consideration—the Apennines of central-southern Italy—a re-equilibrium is possible between marginal mountainous and coastal areas developed through wine–food tourism. It has been demonstrated how there is an important and conscious, although not numerous, productive compartment, how there are motivated and innovative entrepreneurs, despite a public sector that is not always up to the situation. It has been explained how tourism is linked with quality agriculture not only as an economic lever but also as a form of protection of a territory which is fragile and at risk, a contemporary form of sustainable development. It has been pointed out how the sector is taking its first steps and is in an ascending phase in which public support is necessary. A support, however, that should present itself as subsidiary and complementary, according to a bottom-up approach to the problems.

The research has demonstrated that the tradition of quality food is diffused in the internal areas of central Italy. But only in few cases, food and tourism are part of a systemic network of production; tourism alone is not able to increase the value of quality food. For tourist use, it is necessary to tie up the quality food to its "terroir" in such a way that the relationship product—place of production becomes indissoluble. The link with "terroir" is solid if the concept of an integrated food production chain imposes itself. The cooperation within the production chain can be successful only if the "terroir" stakeholders are cooperating among themselves and share the same targets.

The research presented in this paper has shown that

(1) the relationship between quality food and tourism is a lever for local development in marginal areas;
(2) this development is sustainable because of its intrinsic nature: preserving traditional products, traditional landscape, using traditional ways of production, brings sustainability, the long history of traditions is the guarantee of sustainability;
(3) those processes allow the maintenance of environment and the survival of local communities that, in other situations, would be pushed away from marginal areas;
(4) the survival of local communities gives chance to new creative classes to emerge; these new young creations will emerge since they have to satisfy the needs of postmodern tourists or they would not survive;
(5) those processes of development should be sustained by public actors through a bottom-up approach;
(6) development is as such if quality food and tourism are strictly linked to territory and if they respect its peculiarities.

Note

1. Although this paper is a joint work by the two authors, *B. Staniscia* wrote Section 3 and *A. Montanari* wrote the rest.

References

Armesto López, X. A. & Gómez Martín, B. (2006) Tourism and quality agro-food products: An opportunity for the Spanish countryside, *Tijdschrift voor Economische en Sociale Geografie*, 97(2), pp. 166–177.
Augé, M. (1995) *Non-Places: Introduction to an Anthropology of Supermodernity* (London: Verso).
Belisle, F. J. (1983) Tourism and food production in the Caribbean, *Annals of Tourism Research*, 10(3), pp. 497–513.
Bessière, J. (1998) Local development and heritage: Traditional food and cuisine as tourist attractions in rural areas, *Sociologia Ruralis*, 38(1), pp. 21–34.
Che, D. (2006) Select Michigan: Local food production, food safety, culinary heritage, and branding in Michigan agritourism, *Tourism Review International*, 9(4), pp. 349–363.

Cohen, E. & Avieli, N. (2004) Food in tourism: Attraction and impediment, *Annals of Tourism Research*, 31(4), pp. 755–778.

Cortellazzo, M. & Zolli, P. (1999) *DELI, Dizionario etimologico della lingua italiana* (Bologna: Zanichelli).

Fabbris, L. (1991) Problemi statistici nella utilizzazione di dati rilevati presso testimoni privilegiati, in: L. Fabbris (Ed.) *Rilevazioni per campione delle opinioni degli italiani*, pp. 89–115 (Padova: SGE).

Fallon, L. D. & Kriwoken, L. K. (2003) Community involvement in tourism infrastructure: The case of the Strahan Visitor Centre, Tasmania, *Tourism Management*, 24(3), pp. 289–308.

Fawcett, C. & Cormack, P. (2001) Guarding authenticity at literary tourism sites, *Annals of Tourism Research*, 28(3), pp. 686–704.

Feagan, R. (2007) The place of food: Mapping out the "local" in local food systems, *Progress in Human Geography*, 31(1), pp. 23–42.

Florida, R. (2005) *Cities and the Creative Class* (New York: Routledge).

Glenn, J. C. (1999) Participatory methods, in: J. C. Glenn (Ed.) *Futures Research Methodology. The Millennium Project*, Chapter 14 (Washington, DC: American Council for the United Nations University).

Gordon, T. G. & Glenn, J. (1999) Environmental scanning, in: J. C. Glenn (Ed.) *Futures Research Methodology. The Millennium Project*, Chapter 2 (Washington, DC: American Council for the United Nations University).

Hall, M. C. (2006) Introduction. Culinary tourism and regional development: From slow food to slow tourism? *Tourism Review International*, 9(4), pp. 303–305.

Hall, C. M., Sharples, L. & Smith, A. (2003) The experience of consumption or the consumption of experiences? Challenges and issues in food tourism, in: C. M. Hall, L. Sharples, R. Mitchell, B. Cambourne & N. Macionis (Eds) *Food Tourism Around the World: Development, Management and Markets*, pp. 314–315 (Butterworth-Heinemann: Oxford).

Holloway, L., Cox, R., Venn, L., Kneafsey, M., Dowler, E. & Toumaninen, H. (2006) Managing sustainable farmed landscape through "alternative" food networks: A case study from Italy, *The Geographical Journal*, 172(3), pp. 219–220.

Job, H. & Murphy, A. (2006) Germany's Mosel Valley: Can tourism help preserve its cultural heritage? *Tourism Review International*, 9(4), pp. 333–347.

Montanari, A., Costa, N. & Staniscia, B. (2008) *Geografia del gusto. Scenari per l'Abruzzo* (Ortona: Menabò).

Neal, Z. P. (2006) Culinary deserts, gastronomic oases: A classification of US cities, *Urban Studies*, 43(1), pp. 1–21.

Nummendal, M. & Hall, C. M. (2006) Local food in tourism: An investigation of the New Zealand South Islands bed and breakfast sector's use and perception of local food, *Tourism Review International*, 9(4), pp. 365–378.

Pacinelli, A. (2008) *Metodi per la ricerca sociale partecipata* (Milano: Franco Angeli).

Pirog, R. & Paskiet, Z. (2004) *A Geography of Taste: Iowa's Potential for Developing Place-based Traditional Food* (Ames: Iowa State University).

Shortridge, B. G. & Shortridge, J. R. (Eds) (1998) *A Taste of American Place, A Reader on Regional and Ethnic Foods* (Lanham: Rowan & Littlefield).

Socher, K. & Tschurtschenthaler, P. (1994) Tourism and agriculture in Alpine regions, *The Tourist Review*, 49(3), pp. 35–41.

Staniscia, B. (2003) Economic development and international migration in the Sangro Valley, Abruzzo, Italy, *Belgeo*, (1–2), pp. 199–213.

Telfer, D. J. (2001) Strategic alliances along the Niagara Wine Route, *Tourism Management*, 22(1), pp. 21–30.

Telfer, D. J. & Wall, G. (1996) Linkages between tourism and food production, *Annals of Tourism Research*, 23(3), pp. 635–653.

Tremblay, M. (1982) The key informant technique: A non-ethnographic application, in: R. G. Burgess (Ed.) *Field Research: A Sourcebook and Field Manual*, pp. 98–104 (London: George Allen & Unwin).

Tribe, J. (1997) The indiscipline of tourism, *Annals of Tourism Research*, 24(3), pp. 638–657.

Walle, A. H. (1997) Quantitative versus qualitative tourism research, *Annals of Tourism Research*, 24(3), pp. 524–536.

Webb, K. L., Pelletier, D., Maretzki, A. N. & Wilkins, J. (1998) Local food policy coalitions: Evaluation issues as seen by academics, projects organizers, and funders, *Agriculture and Human Values*, 15(1), pp. 65–75.

Weizsäcker, E. U. V., Lovins, A. B. & Lovins, L. H. (1997) *Factor Four. Doubling Wealth—Halving Resource Use* (London: Earthscan).

Working on the Other Side. Cooperative Tour Organizers and Uncooperative Hoteliers: Evidence from Greek Cypriot Tourism Professionals

CRAIG WEBSTER*, BERNARD MUSYCK**, STELIOS ORPHANIDES[†] & DAVID JACOBSON[‡]

*University of Nicosia, Nicosia, Cyprus, **Frederick University, Nicosia, Cyprus, [†]Nicosia, Cyprus, [‡]Dublin City University, Dublin, Ireland

ABSTRACT *In this research, the authors investigate the willingness of the Greek Cypriot tourism professionals to cooperate with the Turkish Cypriot counterparts in the industry. The analytical framework draws on the literature on the conflict in Cyprus, in general, and on the conflict and its impact on tourism, in particular. A few hypotheses are explored relating to what influences the tourism professionals towards cooperating with the Turkish Cypriots: their refugee experience, their increased level of contact with Turkish Cypriots, the size of the organization in which they work and the location and nature of these organizations. The data are based on a series of interviews on the support for cooperation between the tourism professionals among the Greek Cypriots. The findings show that there is clear evidence that the Greek Cypriot hotel managers are unlikely at present to cooperate with the Turkish Cypriot counterparts. On the other hand, the Greek Cypriot tour operators and tourist agencies are willing to collaborate with the other side. This paper follows with a case study of a Greek Cypriot tour-operating company which collaborates with the other side. It is suggested that policies could be designed that aim at the reconciliation of the Greek and Turkish Cypriots through the introduction of political correctness in the business, which is one of the theatres on which the Cyprus conflict is staged.*

Introduction

The Cyprus problem is an issue that has persisted for many years. Since its inception, the Republic of Cyprus has suffered a great deal from its ethnic divisions. The ethnic conflict has resulted in a small island divided into two political entities—one, an internationally recognized republic in which almost all the Greek Cypriots reside, and the other, a state lacking international recognition, in which almost all the Turkish Cypriots reside. The political dividing line is referred to as the "Green Line" (Figure 1).

In this paper, we explore a rather narrow aspect of the Cypriot conflict—the willingness of the Greek Cypriot tourism and hospitality professionals to cooperate with the Turkish Cypriot professionals. The tourism and hospitality industries are very important for both political entities in Cyprus. Because of the ethnic division and continuing animosity in the country, "cooperation with the enemy" is unusual. Yet there is much argument and evidence that cooperation in relation to tourism, where there is inter-communal disagreement, can be advantageous to both sides. The combination of the economic significance of tourism in Cyprus and the paucity of inter-communal cooperation among tourism professionals lends a particular importance to the factors leading to—and impeding—such cooperation.

An example of an impediment was the "ambient atmosphere" (Drousiotis, 2005) in the months following the referendum on the UN plan for the settlement of the Cyprus problem. In October 2004, six months after the referendum, the climate became less favourable for cooperation, as the Greek Cypriot civil society members who participated in the bi-communal projects funded by the United Nations Development Programme were attacked in the media for allegedly having been bribed in order to propagandize in favour of the plan. Although these allegations were at best far-fetched (Drousiotis, 2005), the intensity and the duration of this campaign—which reflected the views of the then President Tassos Papadopoulos—may have further decreased the willingness of the Greek Cypriots to be involved in the bi-communal cooperation.[1] Isolated cases of partnerships in business or of expression of interest in such partnerships also resulted in negative media coverage; this further reduced the willingness of business people to get involved in the bi-communal business cooperation. The survey on which this paper is based was taken on this backdrop. The backdrop suggests one reason why there was so little willingness among the Greek Cypriot tourism professionals to cooperate with their counterparts in the north.[2]

The tourism and hospitality industries in the Republic of Cyprus is important for its economy, as Table 1 illustrates.[3] The general trend shows that arrivals in the past 10

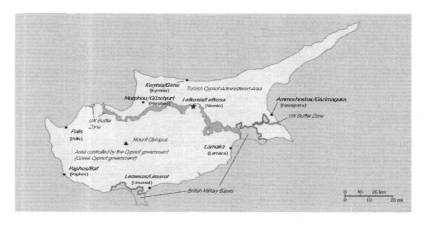

Figure 1. Map of Cyprus
Source: authors' own artwork.

Table 1. Tourism and its contribution to the economy of the Republic of Cyprus

Year	1997	2001	2004	2005	2006	2007
Arrivals	2,088,000	2,696,732	2,349,012	2,470,063	2,400,924	2,416,081
Arrivals annual change (%)	7.1	0.4	2.0	5.2	−2.8	0.6
Revenues from tourism as % of GDP	18.4	20.5	13.3	12.8	12.3	12.0
Real economic growth rate (%)	2.3	4	4.2	3.9	3.8	4.4
Gainful employed (in thousand)	286.2	308.6	322.5	349.5	358.9	369.8
Thereof: hotels and restaurants (in thousand)	29.7	33.5	32.1	35.0	36.0	36.9
As % of total gainful employed	10.4	10.9	10.0	10.0	10.0	10.0

Source: CyStat.

years or so have been on the increase. In addition, there is an indication that the tourism and hospitality industries provide a great deal of employment and revenue. Although the contribution of tourism to GDP has declined over the last decade, at well over 10% it remains extremely significant. It is a key element of the Republic's economy and with the inter-communal cooperation could be even more successful.

Tourism and the related sectors of restaurants and transportation play an important role in the economies of both the south and the north, but more so in the southern part of the island. According to a World Bank report, in 2004 the northern part of Cyprus had about 600,000 tourist arrivals compared with 2.3 million for the southern part of the island. While two-thirds of the tourists visiting the north came from Turkey, the net tourism revenues of USD 288 million far exceeded the USD 62 million revenue for merchandise exports. The contribution of merchandise trade and tourism to GDP was 18% with the share of hotels and restaurants estimated at 3% of GDP (World Bank, 2006, p. 41).

There is a rich body of literature on the tourism industry in the northern part of Cyprus highlighting the difficulties under which the industry has been growing (Lockhart, 1994; Warner, 1999; Altinay, 2000; Altinay & Bowen, 2006; Altinay et al., 2002; Alipour & Kilic, 2005; Altinay & Hussain, 2005; Okumus et al., 2005; Arasli et al., 2006; Gilmore et al., 2007). The main problems discussed in the literature include the international sanctions imposed on the north; the difficulty in achieving a balance between social, economic and environmental perspectives in the regional tourism activities; the lack of a well-formulated policy for the sector and the subsequent need for more state involvement at the strategic level; the lack of professionalism in the industry; the high dependency on Turkish tourists which leads to short, average length of stay, reduced flow of foreign currency and over-reliance on gambling tourism; and various other impediments experienced by the industry due to the unresolved Cyprus problem. The World Bank report (World Bank, 2006) also mentions a few other issues which are closely related to the ones discussed earlier: the problem of unresolved land issues which makes investment in tourism relatively risky and which may explain why currently almost all investment is of local or Turkish origin; the difficulty to promote and market Turkish Cypriot tourism internationally; the fact that hotels operate at a very low capacity;

the large variation of quality in terms of services, food safety standards compliance and accommodation; the inadequacy and high cost of infrastructure (water, electricity and solid waste disposal); a lack of collaboration and commitment by the private and public sector to promote the north as a destination (insufficient professional marketing); and finally, poor land-use planning, which may lead to negative impacts on the prime areas of natural and historic beauty that are the key attractions for tourists.

With this range of research and list of problems in tourism in the north of Cyprus, it is clear that a key impediment to progress is the Cyprus problem. For tourism, the problem is reflected in restrictions on movement, both of tourists and of tourism professionals, across the Green Line. Given the "No" to the Annan Plan in the south, and the "Yes" in the north, the question arises as to whether, in this sector, there is any interest in the south in working with the counterparts in the north.

There are Greek Cypriot professionals in the tourism and hospitality industries who are willing to professionally cooperate with the Turkish Cypriots. However, it is unknown what attributes make persons more willing to cooperate. In this research, we explore those characteristics that seem to be linked with a willingness to cooperate with the Turkish Cypriots on tourism-related issues, in order to learn more about what makes certain individuals more willing to cooperate than others.

To a large extent, the research presented here is inductive and exploratory. While there may be some aspects of the research that are theoretical, the main point of the paper is to find, from the available data, what helps to explain some of the variations in the willingness of the Greek Cypriot professionals in the hospitality and tourism professions to cooperate with the Turkish Cypriot counterparts. The investigation should help shed light on what influences the professionals to be willing to cooperate, and this should provide insights into how cooperation can be fostered and with which segments of the tourism and hospitality professionals such cooperation will meet with the most enthusiasm.

As mentioned earlier, in this paper we followed an inductive and exploratory path. Our initial aim was to test some hypotheses regarding the willingness among the Greek Cypriot tourist professionals to collaborate with their counterparts in the north. Thus, the first part of the project was based on the analysis of quantitative survey results. Through this analysis, we became aware of the particular importance in this context of the role of tour organizers. We therefore decided to carry out a detailed case study of a tour organizer working on both sides of the dividing line. As evidenced later, the tour operator on which we focused our research was the first and only company from the southern part of the island that organized excursions on a regular basis to the northern part of Cyprus. The company has become the undisputed leader in this field and accounts for the large majority of such excursions. The qualitative approach we adopted facilitated an understanding of the exact nature of the cross-border activities of tour operators as well as the potential challenges and opportunities for growth of these collaborative actions. Last but not least, the case study also helped us formulate some policy recommendations.

Thus, from an empirical point of view, the qualitative and quantitative parts of the research supplement each other. Both confirm and reinforce the studied hypotheses and reinforce simultaneously the weight of the main argument developed in this paper. From a methodological point of view, our combined approaches also make sense. The mix of quantitative survey and case study as a means of obtaining primary information is now well established in a variety of literatures. Cooper and Schindler (2008, pp. 185–186), for example, provide a number of instances where this mixed approach—or "triangulation"—is recommended. This includes following a quantitative survey with a case study where further depth is required.

In the next section, we highlight the major academic works on tourism and Cyprus and show how the current literature can be used to inform research on the willingness of people to cooperate across the Green Line. Then, we explain how the data were gathered for the project and the key variables to be explored for the analysis. Next, we explore and analyse the data, using correlations. Before closing the paper, we present a case study of collaboration across the Green Line. To conclude, we discuss what has been learned from the analysis of these data and explain how future research on the topic should proceed.

Literature

The Cyprus Conflict

There is a voluminous literature on Cyprus and the Cyprus conflict.[4] A great deal of the literature, however, only deals with major political issues such as nationalism, and those linked with the country's political division and the Cyprus problem (see, for example, Stavrinides, 1999; Attalides, 1979; Theophanous, 1996, 2000; Joseph, 1997, 1999; Peristianis, 1998; Hutchence & Georgiades, 1999; O'Malley & Craig, 1999; Richmond, 1999; Kyriakou, 2000; Richmond, 2001, 2002; Webster, 2005a, 2005b). A small subset of the literature on Cyprus deals with the topic of the Annan Plan, the UN sponsored plan to reunite the island on a federal basis, on which there was a referendum, on both sides, in 2004 (see, for example, Attalides, 2004; Coufoudakis, 2004; Heraclides, 2004; Jackobsson Hatay, 2004a, 2004b; Christophorou, 2005; Webster & Lordos, 2006). There is also a notable literature looking into the issues linked with the refugees in the Greek Cypriot community (see, for example, Loizos, 1977, 1981; Zetter, 1994; Hadjiyanni, 2001). A few authors use public-opinion approaches to learn more about the general views on these issues (see, for example, Lordos, 2004, 2005a, 2005b; Yildizian & Ehteshami, 2004; Webster, 2005a, 2005b; Webster & Lordos, 2006).

Conflict and Tourism in Cyprus

In contrast to the volume and variety of writing on the Cyprus problem in general, there is relatively little on tourism and the impact of the Cyprus problem on tourism. Clements and Georgiou (1998), in their analysis of "the impact of political instability on a fragile tourism product", show that the dispute between the two communities on the island has been a threat to Cyprus as a tourist destination. Sharpley (2001), too, saw the intensification of the Cyprus problem in 1974, and its aftermath, as having a negative impact on the development of tourism on the island. Further work making similar points includes Ioannides and Apostolopoulos (1999) and Sönmez and Apostolopoulos (2000) on the research on Cyprus and Drakos and Kutan (2003) and Neumayer (2004) on a more general overview of the issue.

The resolution of the Cyprus conflict, according to numerous findings in the literature, would, in general, have a positive effect on the performance of the island's tourism industry. Some go so far as to argue that the very survival of the industry in Cyprus may depend on "promoting a single Cypriot tourism product". To do so, the "two communities need to resolve the prejudices and collaborate toward the creation of a unified and restructured tourism product" (Ioannides & Apostolopoulos, 1999, p. 55). Ioannides and Apostolopoulos (1999) acknowledge that given the differences between the two sides this is a difficult task but they point out that "Despite their political differences, neighbouring countries such as Israel and Egypt feature together in jointly promoted tour packages, especially for long-haul travelers from Japan and the United States" (Ioannides & Apostolopoulos, 1999).

Sönmez and Apostolopoulos (2000) similarly argue that the absence of a symbiosis between the two communities in Cyprus has affected in a negative way the island's ability to compete on the regional and international tourism markets. A stable socio-political climate could have attracted foreign investment and created employment opportunities, and could have improved the chances for further economic development. Altinay and Bowen (2006, p. 952) confirm that tourism and politics seem to strongly interface in the case of Cyprus. While some form of federalism is a highly desirable option, the two sides tend to have different sets of objectives and expectations and there is a general lack of confidence regarding the implementation of a federal solution. "The two societies see themselves as competitors and, more importantly, they do not trust each other... There is little doubt that in the Cyprus case a tourist to the north and south regions would presently receive a two-nation view".

A study on the expected impact of a settlement on the development gap between the two communities was published in 2003 (Ayres, 2003). It was based upon a number of assumptions such as the island's EU membership, the resolution of the property rights issue, the freedom of movement, the existence of a single currency, the provision of financial aid to the Turkish Cypriot economy and the gain of a peace dividend from the demilitarization that would all have a positive effect on the economic growth and employment. The findings were that a solution of the Cyprus problem would benefit the tourism industry of the island as a whole but primarily that of the Turkish Cypriots, as the lifting of the embargo on Ercan airport (the civil airport of the north) and the opening of the whole island to tourists would increase the island's attractiveness to tourists. Tourism in the north, according to Ayres (2003), would then become a driving force for the economy, creating jobs, stimulating investment in new infrastructure and producing rapid growth of tourism receipts. Though assumption rather than analysis, Vassiliou *et al.* (2003) concur with Ayres (2003) in the sense of predicting an improvement of the economic climate, partly as a result of an increase in tourist arrivals and spending, in the event of Annan Plan III being accepted.

Similarly, Eichengreen *et al.* (2004), in the analysis of the prospects of the Turkish Cypriot economy in the case of a settlement, expected a major boost for the tourism industry following the opening up of travel directly to the northern part of the island from outside Cyprus (and Turkey). This study was included in a report prepared for the government of the Republic of Cyprus on the economic aspects of the Annan Plan III. On the other hand, Eichengreen *et al.* (2004) argued that certain provisions of the Plan restricting the mobility of factors such as capital, goods, services, labour and the acquisition of real estate could hamper growth in tourism. Their explanation is that these restrictions could prevent the replication of the "successful model" of the Greek Cypriot tourism development, based on well-managed, small enterprises. The authors indicated that the possible restrictions on the acquisition of property by non-residents could discourage foreign investment and hamper the Turkish Cypriot tourism sector.

These factor mobility restrictions emanated from the bizonal philosophy of the Annan Plan and were not in line with the principles of modern economics, according to

Theophanous (2004). They would have made the viability of the "new" state (sic) uncertain. The resulting political strains would prevent the necessary cooperation between the two communities. The growth potential would not be realized, he argued, because among other things the tourism sector would not be effectively managed.

The boost for the Cypriot tourism sector should not be expected to come only from the traditional markets, as a settlement would lift the political barriers restricting travel from the south to Turkey and vice versa. A study by Mullen *et al.* (2008, p. 29) estimates that in the case of a settlement of the Cyprus problem in 2008, all-Cyprus could expect an annual 30% increase in revenues from Turkish tourists from €178 million in 2006 to €1338 million by 2015. In the no-solution scenario, an annual increase of 9.5% is assumed involving increased revenues from Turkish tourists to €402 million that would flow mainly to the north. A solution would offer all-Cyprus an annual peace dividend in the form of additional spending by Turkish tourists totalling €385 million.

In addition, several studies refer to the region-specific impacts of a political settlement. In a report on the regional tourism strategy for the government-controlled Famagusta area, TTC (2006) estimates that a return of Famagusta to the Greek Cypriots through a political settlement could offer the area an opportunity to create a twenty-first-century holiday resort that would establish itself as the island's primary resort destination.

In a report on the regional tourism strategy for Nicosia, ALA planning partnership (2005) expects very positive and multidimensional effects of political settlement. These would be comparable to the situation that resulted from the partial lifting of restrictions on movements through the Green Line in April 2003; this fuelled the interest of tourists in coastal areas to visit the island's capital on one-day trips. Although Nicosia would not be in position to compete in the mainstream sun and sea product, its uniqueness as a crossroad of cultures, languages and religions, its sightseeing attractions and its vicinity to the northern coast could attract tourists, who might stay in the town for several days.

It follows from this review of the literature that settlement would enhance tourism in Cyprus. Even inter-communal collaboration in current circumstances—i.e. with a number of crossing points across the Green Line—is suggested to be positive for tourism on the island. There is a need, therefore, to investigate willingness to collaborate.

Willingness to Collaborate

There is a great deal written about Cyprus and its major ethnic problem. However, little is known about what makes some citizens more interested in interacting with people across the Green Line than others. Perhaps the most thorough look into interactions using a public-opinion approach is that of Webster (2005a), who investigated the attitude of Greek Cypriots towards interacting with the Turkish Cypriots. The major finding was that there seemed to be something about being in Nicosia or near Nicosia that caused the Greek Cypriots to be more willing to work with, live as neighbours with, share a social life with, inter-marry with, and share businesses with the Turkish Cypriots. What can be extracted from this is that the Greek Cypriots in Nicosia are qualitatively different from other Greek Cypriots, possibly because they live in a more cosmopolitan city, shared with the Turkish Cypriots, but also possibly because they are more likely to interact with the Turkish Cypriots on a regular basis.

Webster (2005a) builds upon the work of Yildizian and Ehteshami (2004), who were testing the idea of the contact hypothesis. The contact hypothesis is the notion that contact with an adversary will lead to humanization of the adversary and thus, an easing of tension. The contact hypothesis is an interesting concept and it can be tested in Cyprus, especially because the liberalization of the crossing points (2003) has given many Cypriots the opportunity to interact, although there is significant evidence that many Greek Cypriots still refuse to cross the Green Line (Webster & Timothy, 2006; Hadjipavlou, 2007).

The published results of a recent bi-communal research project have contributed significantly to the understanding of the nature of the problems faced by the Cypriots who are trying to trade across the Green Line (Hatay *et al.*, 2008). What makes this contribution particularly interesting and original is that besides the analysis of conventional obstacles faced by the traders (red tape, stringent border controls, limited range of tradeable goods, taxation, transportation problems) it also focuses on the opposition to, and the psychological barriers faced by, the entrepreneurs attempting to sell to, and buy from, the other side.

In his review of the earlier-mentioned research, Bahceli (2009, p. 8) describes the trade from the north to the south as an "expensive, time-consuming and demoralizing process" and adds that "the stringent checks at the crossing points tend to remind the Turkish Cypriots of what they recall as the institutionalized persecution and intimidation that foreshadowed the Turkish invasion of 1974". According to the authors of the research, the Turkish Cypriots who are trying to trade across the line share a feeling of "fear of inferiority". "Foremost it is a feeling of numerical inferiority that comes from being a member of a smaller ethnic group. Also, being on the whole less affluent than the Greek Cypriots, coupled with the first or second-hand memory of past victimizations, renders the Green-Line trade a humiliating experience for many" (Bahceli, 2009, p. 8).

On the other hand, among the Greek Cypriots there is the fear that "if they trade, they will be identified and pilloried by their own community, since the produce could involve Greek Cypriot land, which reminds them of the trauma of 1974" (Hatay *et al.*, 2008, p. 1). Thus, according to the authors, there is a tendency towards "denial"; those Greek Cypriots "who do conduct business on the other side feel compelled to deny the existence of their clients or hide their identity by trading only in non-labelled goods" (Hatay *et al.*, 2008). For many Greek Cypriots, doing business across the line is taboo because such dealings may be perceived as not legitimate and may be considered as some form of recognition of the "illegal state". Having said this, the Greek Cypriots have no problems to sell to the Turkish Cypriots, but they do not feel comfortable to buy from them. Incidentally, the Turkish Cypriots drive in large numbers to the south for their grocery shopping but also for consumer durables; buying from Greek Cypriots appears to pose fewer problems to them.

Thus, from a psychological point of view, the Greek Cypriots are guided by a feeling of "denial" while the Turkish Cypriots fear being treated as "inferior"; the overall result is a strong resistance to trade among the Greek Cypriots and a deep resentment about trading among the Turkish Cypriots. Thus, the researchers conclude that to boost trade across the line, the Turkish Cypriots need to be persuaded that what they are doing is perfectly legitimate and is not compromising their self-esteem, while the Greek Cypriots need to feel encouraged by their leaders to be involved in trade and to lift the taboo.

In this work, we investigate some of the major concepts that derive from the literature, mainly in political sciences. First, there is the notion that refugees[5] are different from others. All the major public opinion research relating to political questions on Cyprus use refugee status as an independent variable, because the presumption is that the status shapes an individual's perceptions of political reality. However, refugee status does not always prove to be significant in regressions. The tourism literature (on Cyprus and elsewhere) does not deal with the refugee issue specifically and one of the aims of this paper is to contribute to the literature on this particular aspect. Second, there is the notion that contact with the other major ethnicity on the island shapes perceptions on the desirability of future interactions with the other major ethnicity. Thirdly, there is also the notion that Nicosia is different from other places in Cyprus; it is thought to be more cosmopolitan, bi-communal, and has a different economic basis than the other districts in Cyprus. We also use other available data to learn more about how the Greek Cypriot managers in the tourism sector view interacting with their counterparts on the other side of the Green Line.

Data Gathering

A survey of tourism professionals was carried out in the Republic of Cyprus (the Greek Cypriot side) between June and October 2007.[6] One aim of the survey was to identify the differences between tourism professionals' expectations of tourism business development with and without a solution to the Cyprus problem acceptable to both sides. Another aim was to assess the willingness of each side's tourism professionals to cooperate with those of the other side. There were 91 respondents—owners or managers of 74 hotels and 17 travel agencies. These respondents were tourism professionals found throughout the Republic of Cyprus, in all the districts of the country.

Although the original survey asked a number of questions, it failed to ask some additional questions that were thought to be of interest. For example, it was not thought in the original survey that the refugee status of the respondents would influence the professionals' positions on many of the questions asked. The additional questions asked later were whether the respondent considered himself[7] a refugee, the place of the respondent's residence, whether the respondent had crossed the Green Line to visit the "other" Cyprus, and the location of the company for which the respondent works. One problem with returning to respondents many months later to ask a few key questions was that many of the respondents were not present as many tourism enterprises experience seasonal closures. As a result, there is a great deal of missing data. Of the 91 respondents, 35 respondents could not be contacted.

Measuring the Concepts

The concern in this investigation was to measure the willingness of the Greek Cypriot tourism professionals to cooperate with their Turkish Cypriot counterparts. There are two ways of measuring such cooperation: one, measuring the current cooperation and other, measuring the willingness to cooperate. The question "Are you currently engaged in any tourism activity involving both the North and South of the island?" is used to measure those who currently cooperate with those in the Turkish Republic of Northern Cyprus (TRNC). The responses to the question are shown in Table 2. We see that only a minority (11%) currently cooperates across the Green Line.

Another question measures the willingness to cooperate under current circumstances. The question was "Do you think that, in the event of a continuation of the current situation, there is a possibility of joint tourism activities?" This question taps into whether the current situation is conducive to cooperation. Only 19 of the 91 respondents (about 21% of respondents) said that they feel that there are possibilities to collaborate under

Table 2. Currently cooperating on joint tourism activities

	Frequency	%	Valid %
Valid			
No	81	89.0	89.0
Yes	10	11.0	11.0
Total	91	100.0	100.0

the current circumstances, as shown in Table 3. About 76% responded negatively to the question, showing a great deal of pessimism regarding cooperation.

It is reasonable to expect that the two measures of cooperation mentioned earlier would be highly correlated since they both could be linked with an underlying desire for cooperation across the Green Line. A bivariate correlation of the two variables measuring current cooperation and willingness to cooperate shows that there is inadequate evidence of a strong relationship between the two variables. The Pearson's correlation[8] of the two measures yields only a weak relationship ($r=0.16$) and is only acceptable at a significance level of 0.136 (two-tailed test). What this indicates is that while there is some evidence of a correlation between the two types of cooperation, these two distinct forms of collaboration clearly measure very different things (mainly because they are only correlated at low levels and because the evidence that they are systematically related to each other applies only at a significance level of nearly 0.14). Thus, the measures should be used separately, since they appear to measure two different things.

There are many different attributes one would suspect would be linked with these two variables measuring cooperation. For the independent variables, there were several candidate-variables which we suspected could be promising, but the central one was the link between being a refugee and not. There were also other predictive variables, some of a spatial nature and others denoting types of businesses. Other things were investigated because data permitted it. Thus, some of the research has been inductive and exploratory in its approach, rather than theory-based.

The central focus of this investigation is whether refugees are more willing to cooperate on joint activities than non-refugees. To tap into this concept, we asked recipients whether they consider themselves refugees. Because this question was asked of respondents in a subsequent round of interviews, not all could be contacted. Nevertheless, out of the 91 original interviewees, answers were obtained from 56 (or 62%). Eighteen of those who

Table 3. Willingness to cooperate on joint tourism activities

	Frequency	%	Valid %
Valid			
No	69	75.8	78.4
Yes	19	20.9	21.6
Total	88	96.7	100.0
Missing	3	3.3	
Total	91	100.0	

were contacted said that they are refugees (about 32% of the 56 who were contacted for the follow-up questions), while about 38 (68%) said that they are not refugees.

Another important focus of this investigation is the contact hypothesis—that is the notion that contact with another ethnicity leads to increasing willingness to cooperate. Of all the surveyed businesses, eight businesses reported having Turkish Cypriots on their staff. The expectation, as per the Contact Hypothesis, is that those Greek Cypriot professionals who share their working place with Turkish Cypriot staff will be more likely to welcome increased contacts with Turkish Cypriots professionals in business.

Other factors considered were the type of establishment, the region in which the company is located, the size of the organization and whether the manager who was interviewed had visited the other side of the Green Line. To differentiate between those in the hospitality industry and those in the tourism industry, a dummy variable was used with a "1" denoting those that are hotels, hotel apartments or hotel chains. Those that are not part of the hospitality business (as mentioned earlier) are travel agencies or tour operators (17 out of the 91 interviews). Two regions were marked with dummy variables to denote Nicosia and Paphos (Nicosia is the only land-locked district). The number of employees was used as an additional variable—the smallest organization under study has only four employees while the largest has 550. Finally, to examine the willingness of the manager to cross the Green Line, those who said that they had crossed the Green Line were marked with a dummy variable.

Data Analysis

The small sample size on which this investigation is based limits our ability to perform sophisticated statistical analysis. Since the data are somewhat limited, we opted to use bivariate correlation analysis to see which statistical relationships seem to show a relationship with the relevant dependent variables. Table 4 shows all the computed data.

The findings illustrate that there are certain variables that seem to be correlated with those professionals who presently cooperate. For example, it seems that the larger companies, those companies in Paphos, and hotels are less likely to be cooperating across the Green Line at present. Interestingly, it seems that respondents located in Nicosia are more likely to be cooperating at present.[9] What is noteworthy is that the test of significance for hotels is the most convincing in that the significance level is far below 0.01. Evidence to support the notion that anything else is correlated with the current cooperation is at best weak.

In terms of the gauging of those who are most willing to cooperate under the current circumstances, we see that the presence of Turkish Cypriot employees in the establishment seem to influence the willingness to cooperate, although not in a positive way. More importantly, we see that hotels are less willing to cooperate across the Green Line than other businesses. What is interesting, though, given the contact hypothesis, is that there is strong (statistically significant) evidence that those businesses in Nicosia are more willing to cooperate across the Green Line than businesses in other parts of the country.

Discussion

The findings illustrate several interesting new issues related to the major questions under study. Firstly, there is no evidence that refugee status plays any role in conditioning the

Table 4. Bivariate correlations

	Currently cooperate	Willing to cooperate	Presence of TC employees	Refugee	Number of employees	Nicosia	Paphos	Visited other side	Hotels
Currently cooperate									
Pearson's correlation	1	0.160	0.007	-0.081	-0.193	0.193	-0.186	0.177	-0.553(**)
Significance (two-tailed)		0.136	0.947	0.551	0.066	0.067	0.077	0.192	0.000
N	91	88	85	56	91	91	91	56	91
Willing to cooperate									
Pearson's correlation	0.160	1	-0.181	-0.023	-0.122	0.219(*)	-0.153	0.098	-0.303(**)
Significance (two-tailed)	0.136		0.105	0.866	0.257	0.040	0.155	0.476	0.004
N	88	88	82	55	88	88	88	55	88
Presence of TC employees									
Pearson's correlation	0.007	-0.181	1	-0.076	0.135	0.116	-0.161	0.040	0.060
Significance (two-tailed)	0.947	0.105		0.592	0.217	0.291	0.141	0.777	0.583
N	85	82	85	52	85	85	85	52	85
Refugee									
Pearson's correlation	-0.081	-0.023	-0.076	1	0.025	-0.197	-0.197	0.358(**)	0.052
Significance (two-tailed)	0.551	0.866	0.592		0.857	0.145	0.145	0.007	0.706
N	56	55	52	56	56	56	56	56	56
Number of employees									
Pearson's correlation	-0.193	-0.122	0.135	0.025	1	-0.190	0.225(*)	-0.211	0.292(**)

Significance (two-tailed)	0.066	0.257	0.217	0.857		0.071	0.032	0.118	0.005
N	91	88	85	56	91	91	91	56	91
Nicosia									
Pearson's correlation	0.193	0.219(*)	0.116	−0.197	−0.190	1	−0.197	0.130	−0.514(**)
Significance (two-tailed)	0.067	0.040	0.291	0.145	0.071		0.062	0.338	0.000
N	91	88	85	56	91	91	91	56	91
Paphos									
Pearson's correlation	−0.186	−0.153	−0.161	−0.197	0.225(*)	−0.197	1	−0.316(*)	0.254(*)
Significance (two-tailed)	0.077	0.155	0.141	0.145	0.032	0.062		0.018	0.015
N	91	88	85	56	91	91	91	56	91
Visited other side									
Pearson's correlation	0.177	0.098	0.040	0.358(**)	−0.211	0.130	−0.316(*)	1	−0.117
Significance (two-tailed)	0.192	0.476	0.777	0.007	0.118	0.338	0.018		0.389
N	56	55	52	56	56	56	56	56	56
Hotels									
Pearson's correlation	−0.553(**)	−0.303(**)	0.060	0.052	0.292(**)	−0.514(**)	0.254(*)	−0.117	1
Significance (two-tailed)	0.000	0.004	0.583	0.706	0.005	0.000	0.015	0.389	
N	91	88	85	56	91	91	91	56	91

*Correlation is significant at the 0.05 level (two-tailed).
**Correlation is significant at the 0.01 level (two-tailed).

willingness to cooperate or present cooperation across the Green Line.[10] Secondly, there is only very weak evidence (even with a very liberal view of statistical significance levels) that there is a link between having Turkish Cypriot employees on staff and showing a willingness to cooperate across the Green Line.

An additional finding that seems interesting is that businesses in Nicosia and hotels are distinct in terms of how they view cooperation across the Green Line. For example, we see that respondents based in Nicosia are most likely at present to cooperate (with a liberal view of statistical significance) and are more likely than others to be willing to cooperate across the Green Line. In addition, it seems that hotels are very strongly against cooperation across the Green Line and the levels of statistical significance and correlations show the strongest and clearest systematic relationships of anything investigated with the data available. Hoteliers, it seems, do not cooperate and are not willing to cooperate.[11]

The findings bring up some interesting points for discussion. It seems that the refugee status of the respondent did not play a role in conditioning the current cooperation of the institution nor in the willingness to cooperate. This is interesting because there is research indicating that the refugee status plays an important role in conditioning political action and positions among the Greek Cypriots (see Webster & Lordos, 2006; Webster & Timothy, 2006). In this case, there is no reason to believe that the life experience of being a refugee plays a role in developing a willingness to cooperate across the Green Line.

Even more interestingly, it seems that one test of the contact hypothesis works in a counter-intuitive way, the findings suggest. There is some weak evidence that those Greek Cypriot companies that have Turkish Cypriot employees are somewhat less willing to cooperate across the Green Line. It seems that contact, in this case, does not breed an atmosphere encouraging cooperation; the data suggest it does actually the opposite. It may well be that those Greek Cypriot companies that employ Turkish Cypriots develop a relationship, predominantly boss–worker, with them and that this has fostered a spirit of contempt for the "other". Also, the existence of an atmosphere hostile to cooperation in the years following the referendum may be another explanation. A more pragmatic explanation may simply be that Turkish Cypriot staff are hired by the Greek Cypriot entrepreneurs because they are the cheapest legal and qualified source of labour, indicating that they were employed because of economic necessity rather than ideological preference. They may indeed be reluctant to hire Turkish workers, feel forced to do so, and this offsets the potential for contact to ease tension. At any rate, while there is only weak evidence one way or the other to test the contact hypothesis, we see that in relation to employment, the evidence that exists runs in the direction counter to that expected.

In terms of other hypotheses, two items stand out—Nicosia businesses are different from businesses elsewhere on the island, and hotels have a different stance than do other types of tourism business. The data show that there is some evidence that businesses in Nicosia are more willing than others to cooperate across the Green Line. This is not surprising because there has been evidence that the willingness to interact with Turkish Cypriots seems to be linked with Nicosia (Webster, 2005a). It may well be that Nicosia is qualitatively different from the rest of the country—it is landlocked, it is the capital, it is divided and in many respects, a cosmopolitan place—making residents more willing to interact across an ethnic and political divide. Nicosia has also traditionally been a focal point for many bi-communal projects and events (notably at the

UN-controlled Ledra Palace hotel, which is a neutral meeting place and the Ledra hotel checkpoint, which remained the only gate to the other side for three decades), it has a strong representation of civil society organizations, and last but not least, three convenient crossing points. In recent years, a steady flow of Turkish Cypriot day commuters use the Nicosia checkpoints to go to work on the Greek side, some pupils also attend English schools. Perhaps even more significant is the large number of Turkish Cypriot consumers who visit the Nicosia hypermarkets, DIY and furniture centres, toy stores and shopping malls, on a regular basis.[12] Thus, there is an "air of normality" which results from the comings and goings of Turkish Cypriots across the Green Line, Turkish Cypriot registered cars are seen everywhere in Nicosia and nobody is surprised anymore to hear Turkish spoken in shops and other retail establishments around the capital. Together, all these factors may contribute to make Nicosia different from other towns in Cyprus, but it is unclear from our study what the exact drivers of this tendency are. Ironically, given the finding in relation to the presence of Turkish Cypriot employees, the Nicosia finding seems to support the Contact Hypothesis. There is greater willingness among the Greek Cypriot tourism professionals in Nicosia, who live in closer proximity and have more interaction with Turkish Cypriots, to collaborate with their counterparts in the north. This greater willingness to collaborate may, of course, be because of greater possibility of commercial exploitation of cross-Green Line activity in Nicosia than elsewhere. Further research, identifying the underlying reasons for our findings, may help in formulating future policy.

In terms of the very strong negative reactions regarding cooperation from hoteliers, it seems that the relationship can be explained fairly easily. What differentiates the tourism companies and hospitality institutions seems to be the relationship with ownership of land. Property ownership is a hot issue in Cyprus, since the Cypriots base a great deal of status upon the ownership of land (Zetter, 1994).[13] While the hoteliers make revenue from selling bed-nights in a physical location, the travel agencies make revenue from providing services to tourists. The hoteliers are likely to have responded to questions of cooperation in a defensive way, since many may view their competitors on the other side of the Green Line as making their living off "stolen property" taken from the Greek Cypriots following the 1974 invasion of Cyprus by the Turkish army, with some of these hoteliers being dispossessed owners themselves. Another possible explanation is that the hoteliers may view cooperation as problematic, since hotel bed-nights is a zero sum game; tourists, in most reasonable instances, only use one bed per night. However, the tour agents and tour guides may not perceive their business as a zero-sum game, since it is a business based upon selling of additional and complementary services to the customers. Though these explanations appear sufficient to justify the rejection of horizontal cooperation, they do not necessarily apply in relation to the prospect of vertical cooperation with the Turkish Cypriot travel agencies and tour operators. As the services of the travel agencies and tour operators are not necessarily connected to the land-ownership issue, there could be other causes behind the rejection of potential additional business that remain to be identified.

A main finding of our research is that of the cooperative tour organizers and uncooperative hoteliers. Once this became clear, we continued our inductive research path and decided that we needed to know more about those who were most likely to collaborate with the other side. The next section of the article presents a case study of a Greek Cypriot travel agency and tour-operator, which has been involved since 2003 in collaborative work across the Green Line. The analysis offers a reflection on the challenges faced by such collaboration and the opportunities that may (or may not) open in the future. At the back of our mind lies the idea that collaboration in the tourism sector may lead the way to further positive developments for other areas of the island's economy and society.

A Cooperative Tour Operator—Case Study

Evidence was collected from the major tour company operating on the island (Papageorgiou, 2008).[14] The tour operator called AEOLOS is partly owned by a local investor's group (Frangoudi & Stephanou) and is part of one of Europe's largest tour operators, TUI Travel Plc, essentially a British company. The Cyprus operations of the company account for about 25% of the island's market of incoming tourists (over half a million tourists per year). AEOLOS was the first and only company from the southern part of Cyprus that organized excursions on a regular basis to the northern part of Cyprus, soon after Green Line crossing became possible in April 2003. The company became and is still the undisputed leader in this field, with about 20–30 buses crossing the Green Line from the south every week. (Other companies together account for no more than half a dozen coaches per week). Excursions are organized from the south to Kyrenia, Famagusta and northern Nicosia. There are no excursions organized from the north to the south because the majority of tourists visiting the north come from Turkey and are not allowed to cross the Green Line according to the Green-Line regulation. The English and other foreign clientele in the north who technically would be allowed to cross the Green Line do not, in terms of numbers, justify regular excursions across the line.

Initially AEOLOS expected that the business in the north would develop very fast and that soon after organizing day trips the company would develop further products involving overnight stays and more sophisticated services. However, this did not take place because it became apparent that the company could not afford the complexity required in doing business in the north. As a mass tourism operator, AEOLOS is trying to reduce complexities and simplify communication in search of cost effectiveness. The major problem that the company encountered in the north is related to liability issues. It considered that the current legal framework in the north did not allow it to send big volumes of clients without running the risk of facing major difficulties "in case something happens". Customers can get sick, have accidents and even die while on holiday, and this leads to a whole range of formalities, which are the responsibilities of the tour operator. In case of such complications, the fact that services are rendered in a geographical entity which "suffers from a legal void" (the TRNC is not recognized by any country except Turkey and thus, does not host any diplomatic representations and does not maintain any official relations with other countries) may create substantial additional problems with possible grave consequences. Thus, according to the tour operator, the fact that business so far has not expanded beyond the organization of day trips across the Green Line is not linked to a lack of commercial interest,[15] but has more to do with issues related to customers' safety.

Having said this, according to the tour operator, the cost of the excursion is increasing because official regulation requires that each coach be accompanied by an accredited local tour guide.[16] The same regulation is enforced on both sides of the Green Line, by both separate administrations, which means that every coach always carries two official guides, at least while operating in the northern part of the island. An additional problem is that official tour guides are often "patriotic" and "biased" when it comes to discussing politically sensitive issues.[17] Thus, the tour operator has to provide the guides with clear specifications of the tour, instruct them to adopt a moderate approach towards the subject because clients on such tours do not want to hear political propaganda; they want to be informed. It is also often the case that both official guides participate passively in the excursion while a guide working for the tour operator (who is then a third guide on the coach!) does all the work. This happens when coaches are organized for clients speaking languages not covered by official guides (Finnish and Swedish, for instance). AEOLOS is the largest employer of official tour guides in Cyprus, and payment for official guiding services represent a substantial cost for the company. Among the problems encountered in the north is the huge entrance fees of museum and archaeological sites.

Excursions to the north (to the costal towns of Kyrenia and Famagusta) have reached a stage of product maturity; they are no longer growing. The lack of novelty of the product, change in fashion, decreased interest by the media, swing in the overall demand and general decline of tourism business in the south have all taken their toll on the business. Since the opening of the Ledra street checkpoint in Nicosia (a highly symbolic event since historically Ledra street had been the main shopping artery of the capital and had been divided since the 1960s) in the spring of 2008, the tour company is now offering a new product which has proved rather successful (a frequency of 10–20 buses per week depending on the season). The "Nicosia Mix 'n Match" excursion brings tourists to the capital and guides them in a walk across the divided city through the Ledra street checkpoint. A guided walk on both sides of the dividing line allows the tourists to get a "feel" for the two sides and gain a unique experience of the diversity that Cyprus can offer. The tourists are invited to walk within the unified space of the old walled city of Nicosia to discover a variety of architecture, culture, language, religion, people, food and atmosphere. Of course, a sizeable proportion of these tourists are also interested in political tourism[18] as documented by the works of Lisle (2007) and Leonard (2007) in Nicosia. Lisle notes that in the context of the opening of Ledra Street, "political tourism is significant because it forces divided societies to confront the difficult issue of "where" and "how" to represent their dissonant heritage in a way that satisfies both local communities and international visitors. This process—as well as political tourism's participation in it—is crucial to any context of peace and reconciliation" (2007, p. 109).

She adds that "the representations of conflict in Cyprus—either outdated propaganda in the North or nostalgic erasure in the South—have shown to be insufficient in a context where locals and tourists can cross the border reasonably freely. As the drive for reconciliation gains momentum, these radically incompatible representations of Cypriot history will become increasingly obsolete" (2007, p. 112).

In a sense, this excursion may represent what Cyprus would have to offer if it were a unified island. Such an island would represent a totally different attraction for tour operators. Besides the variety of facets described earlier, the pristine landscape in the north would find a perfect match with the high end of the market and sophisticated clientele currently visiting the south.[19] Clients that visit the south are increasingly environmentally conscious and also well educated.

Two main lessons—a pessimistic and an optimistic one—can be drawn from the professional tour operator's perspective. From a realistic (or pessimistic) point of view, it seems that unless the political situation changes, not much may change in the business; in fact "southern" business activities in the north might even regress in the medium term once the novelty of the day trips to the north disappears. For such a tourist-activity volume to take off in the north, there needs to be a proper framework that addresses all the pending issues of liability, safety, hygiene, legal issues, accountability, etc. Arguably reconciliation cannot grow out of collaboration because no further collaboration can take place until the political problem is solved. The impediments to growth in the north from a tour operator's perspective are not linked to the economic or commercial issues but are dependent on a series of institutional and legal factors.

In other words, there is ample interest from the large European tour operators to further develop their business in the north from their bases in the south or even directly, but business will not be able to take off if the political problem is not solved first. Thus, the only form of significant collaboration that will remain is the daily visit by the tourists (study tours—even with overnight stays in the north—could be organized in small numbers but given all the legal problems will never reach the tourist volume of the day excursions). The volume market of tourists which has been the engine of growth of the tourism sector in the south for the last three decades will not be able to contribute substantially to the economic growth the north as long as the large tour operators do not find an adequate operating environment in the north.

In contrast, it could be argued that successful companies do not wait for the political solutions before seizing the commercial opportunities. They can even pursue their commercial interests by promoting reconciliation through collaboration.[20] From the Greek Cypriot tour operator's perspective, a practical step in this direction would be to push for a regulatory change that allows excursions to use only one guide per coach (the same accredited guide would be in charge of the excursion both north and south of the line). This regulatory change may offer a reduction in operating costs and reduce the risk of "political partiality" during the guided visits.[21] A common island-wide scheme of qualifying and accrediting guides originating from both the south and the north may be an over-ambitious aim that would require a substantial collaboration between the two sides. However, the tourist operators on both sides of the dividing line may be interested in promoting the idea of information standards across the value chain (guides, hotels, catering, tourist agencies) to avoid exposing the tourists to any sort of propaganda. As one tour operator put it "we should not use customers who are buying services from our industry to tell them something they don't want to hear".[22] The political situation in Cyprus so far has been an impediment to creating a common language for tour guides, acceptable to both sides of the conflict.

Conclusion

The findings from our analysis provide insights into what is currently happening in Cyprus and suggestions for future research. We learned that refugees do not appear to view cooperation across the Green Line differently from others and there is some weak evidence that having the Turkish Cypriots on staff undermines a willingness to cooperate with Turkish Cypriots in business. Further research should look into whether this relationship holds up in the future. Both findings are contrary to our initial expectations following the hypotheses we had set.

The other findings are the uniqueness of businesses in Nicosia and hotels. Future research might identify the underlying reasons for the greater willingness of businesses in Nicosia to cooperate with the Turkish Cypriots. Regarding hoteliers, it would be interesting to determine whether the Greek Cypriot hoteliers reject horizontal and vertical cooperation and the reasons behind the rejection of cooperation with the Turkish Cypriot travel agents and tour operators. The most logical follow-up would be to have in-depth interviews with the hoteliers and travel agencies to learn more about how they perceive each other and how they view possible collaborations. Additional fieldwork may also examine the effect of the political climate on the opinions of professionals, as shaped by the stance of the political leadership towards cooperation with the Turkish Cypriots. In fact, the survey was carried out before the change of government in the south and since the coalition led by Mr. Christofias took power, there has been a revival of "rapprochement" activities promoted by the civil society and other bi-communal groups.

From the case study, we learn that it has been possible to organize profitable cross-Green Line tourist activities; this may well explain the greater willingness among the tourist agencies to cooperate with the counterparts in the north. However, the companies already involved in business across the line will not be able, under current circumstances, to expand such activities far beyond what has already been achieved. Further development of this sector will require the acceptance of regulatory changes in both the north and the south for example in relation to tour guides. Attitudinal changes will also be necessary before such changes can be achieved, for example, in relation to the standard content of the courses that tour guides require for certification.

Some reservations about our findings are appropriate. The sample size is rather small (only 91). This affects the statistical relationships between the variables. The empty-cell problem arises particularly in relation to those questions that were asked after the original interviews, since so many of the responses are missing.

However, despite these weaknesses, an important outcome is that this study suggests that the tourism agencies and tour operators will be the most fruitful actors in terms of fostering cooperation between tourism professionals in the two entities in Cyprus in the event of a settlement. Although it is still somewhat unclear why they are different from the hoteliers, we see that their willingness to collaborate is greater than that of the hoteliers.

The nature and findings of this research will be relevant to the researchers and practitioners interested in whether the tourism sector can support cooperation between the two communities on the island. Our work, and follow-on research along similar lines, can inform policy in the future. We have contributed to a better understanding of how to stimulate tourism "across the line". This may prove to be particularly relevant within the context of the recent, renewed efforts to solve the Cyprus problem.

Acknowledgements

This study was part of a joined study (Mehmet *et al.*, 2008) in which an identical questionnaire was used both for Turkish Cypriot and for Greek Cypriot tourism professionals. This paper reports on the Greek Cypriot part of the survey.

Notes

1. The defamation campaign was directed mainly against the politicians and journalists who expressed support for the UN plan in the run up to the referendum, though single members of the civil society had also been targeted (see Drousiotis, 2005).
2. There are prominent cases of individuals who demonstrated interest in bi-communal business cooperation which received negative press coverage. For example, Vassiliko Cement Works (in Greek Cypriot south) was interested in selling cement to Turkish Cypriot buyers (http://www.

simerini.com/nqcontent.cfm?a_id=159480) and a company was established by ex-minister of Agriculture Costas Themistocleous with Turkish Cypriot partners (http://www.hri.org/cgi-bin/ brief?/news/cyprus/kypegr/2005/05-06-11.kypegr.html).

3. According to Eurostat, Cyprus has also a relatively large bed capacity compared to its population (115 per 1000 inhabitants in 2006). For comparison, France has 20 beds per 1000 inhabitants, Greece 62, Italy 35 and Spain 37.

4. For those who want to investigate the size of the literature written on the Cyprus conflict, Demetriou's (2004) article is a good introduction.

5. The term refugee applied in this document refers to dislocated Greek Cypriots who lived prior to the 1974 events north of the demarcation line and their descendants.

6. Detailed survey material can be found in Mehmet *et al.* (2008).

7. The respondents were predominantly male.

8. Other measures of correlation were also used in this diagnostic analysis (Kendall's Tau and Spearman's Rho). The correlation coefficients and significance levels using these alternative measures were almost identical to those derived from the Pearson approach.

9. This is consistent with the analysis of the results of the 2004 referendum on the Annan plan, which shows an increase in the negative vote, which is positively correlated with distance from the dividing line (70% rejection in Nicosia against 82% in Paphos—Christophorou, 2005, p. 97).

10. Similar findings confirming the non-relevance of the refugee status have also been reported in the literature within different research contexts. In her work on the crossings of the Green Line, Hadjipavlou (2007, p. 69) indicates that "The crossings do carry personal, political and social meanings which vary among the different social groups cutting across ideologies, class, age and refugee or non-refugee identity". Similarly, in his study of the background of the referenda in Cyprus on the Annan Plan, Christophorou (2005, p. 97) notes that "At first sight, it appeared that the Greek Cypriot refugees, who fled the north of the island during and following the advance of the Turkish Army in summer 1974 had similar attitudes to the rest of the population. It appears that the vast majority viewed the return of territory and about half of the refugees to their homes, under Greek Cypriot control, as insufficient reason to support the plan".

11. Over 97% of the hoteliers in our sample are not currently cooperating across the Green Line, while the corresponding figure for non-hoteliers is about 53%.

12. Mullen (2008, p. 3) reports that:

Greek Cypriot businesses appear to be the net beneficiaries of the opening of the Green Line in April 2003, as total spending by Turkish Cypriots in the south reached EUR 14.3 mln in January-September, whereas total spending by Greek Cypriots reached only around EUR 5.5 mln, according to the JCC [credit card clearing house] joint venture run by the commercial banks. The largest beneficiary of spending using Turkish credit cards in the south was supermarkets, earning EUR 3.4 mln, followed by clothing (EUR 2.8 mln), "other retailers" (EUR 2.08 mln) and DIY and household stores (EUR 2.06 mln).

13. Hadjipavlou (2007, p. 64) adds:

The property issue is the most complex and significant one in the Cyprus conflict because of its connection to identity, justice and family history. This complexity emerged during the 'crossings'. This is an example where the same space, a family house, provides for and symbolizes past and present memories and realities. Both parties legitimately claim it to be their own. These individuals shared personal stories related to the same piece of land, which violence and war took its past owner and handed it to the present one. They both experienced dislocation and fear.

14. Except where otherwise indicated, this section—and any quotes in it—are drawn from personal communication with Mrs. Papageorgiou.

15. From a commercial point of view, the tour operator collaborates with a Turkish Cypriot company, which takes care of all the details of the operations in the north. As it stands today, this collaboration is smooth and requires communication with only one partner and the excursion is reported to be an interesting product offering a high yield.

16. When several coaches are re-united for the purpose of a guided visit at a given tourist spot, the "one coach-one guide" rule is still strictly enforced. It can be argued that the guides in the south operate with a kind of "closed shop mentality" and are highly regulated by their own association (the Cyprus Tourist Guides Association—CTGA) and the Cyprus Tourism Organisation. The guides are seen to protect their monopoly in the market, partly by imposing Greek as an obligatory language for accredited guides while in fact it is the least used language in the market.

17. According to Leonard (2007, p. 69),

> As with the Turkish Cypriot tour guides, the Greek Cypriot guides claim that their tours are histori-cal, however, the over-emphasis of certain historical events and neglect of others is a deeply political act enabling guides from both sides of Nicosia to present a partial view of history favourable to a specific biased interpretation of the conflict. Hence both Greek and Turkish Cypriots hope to gain more political sympathy with their struggle by exposing tourists to certain dimensions of the conflict. Moreover, as with the Turkish Cypriot guide, during informal conversations, both Greek Cypriot guides draw poignantly on their personal history of losing their former homes in the North adding credibility to their subsequent interpretation of the contested nature of their country.

18. On political tourism see also other relevant contributions in Israel and Ireland by Brin (2006), Gelbman (2008), and McDowell (2008).

19. Altinay and Bowen (2006, p. 953) concur with the view that diversity will be the asset of the new Cyprus: ". . . both mistrust and negative competition would lose some of their venom if the Cyprus product could be viewed as diversified: not out of neglect or lack of political power, but out of a sensible island-wide strategy to encourage breadth in the product offering".

20. Others have also echoed this view. Altinay and Bowen (2006, p. 953) indicate that "a political solution in Cyprus requires appropriate preparation of both the national and the operating environment of the country even before a federal solution is established". Hadjipavlou (2007, p. 62) makes the same argu-ment in a more forceful way: "In fact, the state has undermined the importance of reconciliation by insisting that there can be no reconciliation prior to a solution. From my research, I find that the recon-ciliation processes need to start in parallel to the official negotiations. People need to be socialized in a culture of safety, trust and confidence in the future so that they can invest in the implementation of the political solution when it comes". Christophorou (2005, p. 102) explains the rejection of the Annan peace plan with a range of reasons including the fact that "nothing substantial had been done to prepare the Greek Cypriots for reconciliation, to face the realities of a federal solution, and, especially, to come to terms with the radical changes that time has brought to all aspects of life on the island". Still, we should not ignore efforts that are being made by the Greek Cypriot minister of Education Mr. Andreas Demetriou as well as the steps that have already been taken by the TRNC government under pro-reunification Turkish Republican Party (CTP) in reviewing the content of the respective schoolbooks on the history of Cyprus in an attempt to promote reconciliation and empathy with the other side (see also Papadakis, 2008). These attempts may also serve as a basis for reviewing the content of tourist brochures or the information given by tourist guides.

21. "While tourists are not passive recipients of dominant discourses, for a short period of time they provide a captive audience which can be influenced, persuaded, cajoled and deceived into accepting the legiti-macy of certain interpretations of events over others" (Leonard, 2007, p. 72).

22. This is also evidenced by a letter sent to the editor of the Sunday Mail, the main English language news-paper published in Nicosia. The letter was entitled "Tourists don't want a Cyprus problem lecture" (Winnett, 2008).

References

ALA Planning Partnership (2005) *Regional Tourism Strategy Study for Nicosia – Final Strategy Study* Nicosia (published in Greek: Περιφερειακή Στρατηγική Τουρισμού Πόλης και Επαρχίας Λευκωσίας – Τελική Μελέτη Στρατηγικής).

Alipour, H. & Kilic, H. (2005) An institutional appraisal of tourism development and planning: The case of the Turkish republic of north Cyprus (TRNC), *Tourism Management*, 26(1), pp. 79–94.

Altinay, L. (2000) Possible impacts of a federal solution to the Cyprus problem on the tourism industry of north Cyprus, *International Journal of Hospitality Management*, 19(3), pp. 295–309.

Altinay, L. & Bowen, D. (2006) Politics and tourism interface. The case of Cyprus, *Annals of Tourism Research*, 33(40), pp. 939–956.

Altinay, L., Altinay, M. & Bicak, H. A. (2002) Political scenarios: The future of the north Cyprus tourism industry, *International Journal of Contemporary Hospitality Management*, 14(4), pp. 176–182.

Altinay, M. & Hussain, K. (2005) Sustainable tourism development: A case study of north Cyprus, *International Journal of Contemporary Hospitality Management*, 17(3), pp. 272–280.

Arasli, H., Bavik, A. & Ekiz, E. (2006) The effects of nepotism on human resource management. The case of three, four and five star hotels in northern Cyprus, *International Journal of Sociology and Social Policy*, 26(7/8), pp. 295–308.

Attalides, M. (1979) *Cyprus, Nationalism and International Politics* (New York: St. Martin's Press).

Attalides, M. (2004) The political process in Cyprus and the day after the referendum, *The Cyprus Review*, 16(1), pp. 137–146.

Ayres, R. (2003) The economic costs of separation: The north–south development gap in Cyprus, *Ekonomia*, 6(1), pp. 39–52.

Bahceli, S. (2009) Trading the way to a solution: A new study shows Greek and Turkish Cypriots are still very resistant to doing business with each other, *Sunday Mail (Cyprus Mail)*, January 4, pp. 8–9.

Brin, E. (2006) Politically-orientated tourism in Jerusalem, *Tourist Studies*, 6(3), pp. 215–243.

Christophorou, C. (2005) The vote for a united Cyprus deepens divisions: The 24 April 2004 referenda in Cyprus, *South European Society and Politics*, 10(1), pp. 85–104.

Clements, M. A. & Georgiou, A. (1998) The impact of political instability on a fragile tourism product, *Tourism Management*, 19(3), pp. 283–288.

Cooper, D. R. & Schindler, P. S. (2008) *Business Research Methods* (New York: McGraw-Hill).

Coufoudakis, V. (2004) Cyprus – the referendum and its aftermath, *The Cyprus Review*, 16(2), pp. 67–82.

Demetriou, O. (2004) *EU and the Cyprus conflict: Review of the literature*, The European Union and Border Conflicts Working Paper No 5, January, University of Birmingham, UK: EUBorderConf. Available at http://www.euborderconf.bham.ac.uk/publications/files/WP5Cyprus.pdf (accessed 22 July 2009).

Drakos, K. & Kutan, A. (2003) Regional effects of terrorism on tourism in three mediterranean countries, *Journal of Conflict Resolution*, 47(5), pp. 621–641.

Drousiotis, M. (2005) *The Ambient Atmosphere – The Obliteration of Opposing Opinion through Defamation: The Case of President Papadopoulos' Accusations that his Political Opponents were Financed by the United States and the United Nations,* Nicosia: IKME.

Eichengreen, B., Faini, R., von Hagen, J. & Wyplosz, C. (2004) *Economic Aspects of the Annan Plan for the Solution of the Cyprus Problem*, Report to Government of the Republic of Cyprus, February 17, Nicosia.

Gelbman, A. (2008) Border tourism in Israel: Conflict, peace, fear and hope, *Tourism Geographies*, 10(2), pp. 193–213.

Gilmore, A., Carson, D., Fawcett, L. & Ascenção, M. (2007) Sustainable marketing – the case of northern Cyprus, *The Marketing Review*, 7(2), pp. 113–124.

Hadjipavlou, M. (2007) Multiple stories: The 'crossings' as part of citizen's reconciliation efforts in Cyprus? *Innovation*, 20(1), pp. 53–73.

Hadjiyanni, T. (2001) The persistence of refugee consciousness—the case of Greek-Cypriot refugees, *The Cyprus Review*, 13(2), pp. 93–110.

Hatay, M., Mullen, F. & Kalimeri, J. (2008) *Intra-Island Trade in Cyprus: Obstacles, Oppositions and Psychological Barriers*, Paper 2/2008, Nicosia: PRIO Cyprus Centre.

Heraclides, A. (2004) The Cyprus problem and open and shut case? Probing the Greek-Cypriot rejection of the Annan plan, *The Cyprus Review*, 16(2), pp. 37–54.

Hutchence, J. & Georgiades, H. (1999) The European union and the Cyprus problem: Powerless to help? *The Cyprus Review*, 11(1), pp. 83–96.

Ioannides, D. & Apostolopoulos, Y. (1999) Political instability, war, and tourism in Cyprus: Effects, management, and prospects for recovery, *Journal of Travel Research*, 38(1), pp. 51–56.

Jackobsson Hatay, A. (2004a) Popular referenda and peace processes: The twin referenda on the Annan plan for a reunited Cyprus put in perspective, *Turkish Daily News*, May 4–6, 2004.

Jackobsson Hatay, A. (2004b) *The people deliver their verdict on the Annan plan for a re-united Cyprus*. Sweden: The Transnational Foundation for Peace and Future Research. Available at http://www.transnational.org/forum/meet/2004/Jak_Hatay_CyprusRef.html (accessed 22 July 2009).

Joseph, J. (1997) *Cyprus: Ethnic Conflict and International Politics, From Independence to the Threshold of the European Union* (London/New York: Macmillan Press/St. Martin's Press).

Joseph, J. (1999) Cyprus and the EU: Searching for a settlement in the light of accession, *The Cyprus Review*, 11(1), pp. 33–57.

Kyriacou, A. (2000) A just and lasting solution to the Cyprus problem: In search of institutional viability, *Mediterranean Politics*, 5(30), pp. 54–75.

Leonard, M. (2007) A little bit of history and a lot of opinion: Biased authenticity in Belfast and Nicosia, *Journal of Cyprus Studies*, 13(32–33), pp. 53–77.

Lisle, D. (2007) Encounters with partition: Tourism and reconciliation in Cyprus, in: L. Purbrick, J. Aulich & G. Dawson (Eds) *Contested Spaces: Sites, Representations and Histories of Conflict* (Basingstoke: Palgrave).

Lockhart, D. (1994) Tourism in Northern Cyprus: Patterns, policies and prospects, *Tourism Management*, 15(5), pp. 370–400.

Loizos, P. (1977) Argaki, the uprooting of a Cypriot village, in: M. Attalides (Ed.) *Cyprus Reviewed* (Nicosia: The Jus Cypria Association and the Coordinating Committee of Scientific and Cultural Organizations).

Loizos, P. (1981) *The Heart Grown Bitter: A Chronicle of Cypriot War Refugees* (Cambridge: Cambridge University Press).

Lordos, A. (2004) Can the Cyprus Problem be Solved?. Available at http://www.cypruspolls.org (accessed 22 July 2009).

Lordos, A. (2005a) Civil Society Diplomacy: A New Approach for Cyprus. Available at http://www.help-net.gr/download.htm (accessed 22 July 2009).

Lordos, A. (2005b) Options for Peace: Mapping the Possibilities for a Comprehensive Settlement in Cyprus. Available at http://www.cypruspolls.org (accessed 22 July 2009).

McDowell, S. (2008) Selling conflict heritage through tourism in peacetime Northern Ireland: Transforming conflict or exacerbating differences? *International Journal of Heritage Studies*, 14(5), pp. 405–421.

Mehmet, O., Jacobson, D., Yorucu, V., Orphanides, S., Michaelides, G., Katircioglu, S., Webster, C., Musyck, B., Violaris, J. & Tahiroglu, M. (2008) *The Future of the Tourism Industry in Cyprus: Divided or Reunited?*, Monograph (Nicosia: The Management Centre of the Mediterranean).

Mullen, F. (2008) Greek Cypriot businesses net beneficiaries of Green Line, Local credit card use up 20% in Jan–Sep, *Financial Mirror*, October 29.

Mullen, F., Oğuz, Ö. & Antoniadou-Kyriakou, P. (2008) *The Day After – Commercial Opportunities after a Solution to the Cyprus Problem* (Nicosia: Peace Research Institute Oslo, Cyprus Centre).

Neumayer, R. (2004) The impact of political violence on tourism. Dynamic cross-national estimation, *Journal of Conflict Resolution*, 48(2), pp. 259–281.

Okumus, F., Altinay, M. & Arasli, H. (2005) The impact of Turkey's economic crisis of February 2001 on the tourism industry in Northern Cyprus, *Tourism Management*, 26(1), pp. 95–104.

O'Malley, B. & Craig, I. (1999) *The Cyprus Conspiracy: America, Espionage, and the Turkish Invasion* (London: IB Tauris).

Papadakis, Y. (2008) *History Education in Divided Cyprus: A Comparison of Greek Cypriot and Turkish Cypriot Schoolbooks on the "History of Cyprus"* (Nicosia: Peace Research Institute Oslo, Cyprus Centre).

Papageorgiou, A. (2008) Personal communication, General Manager Incoming Department AEOLOS tour operator, 20 October, Nicosia.

Peristianis, N. (1998) A federal Cyprus in a federal Europe, *The Cyprus Review*, 10(1), pp. 33–43.

Richmond, O. (1999) Ethno-nationalism, sovereignty and negotiating positions in the Cyprus conflict: Obstacles to a settlement, *Middle East Studies*, 35(3), pp. 42–63.

Richmond, O. (2001) A perilous catalyst? EU accession and the Cyprus problem, *The Cyprus Review*, 13(2), pp. 123–132.

Richmond, O. (2002) Decolonisation and post-independence cause of conflict: The case of Cyprus, *Civil Wars*, 5(3), pp. 163–190.

Sharpley, R. (2001) Tourism in Cyprus: Challenges and opportunities, *Tourism Geographies*, 3(1), pp. 64–86.

Sönmez, S. & Apostolopoulos, Y. (2000) Conflict resolution through tourism cooperation? The case of the partitioned island-state of Cyprus, *Journal of Travel & Tourism Marketing*, 9(3), pp. 35–48.

Stavrinides, Z. (1999) *The Cyprus Conflict: National Identity and Statehood*, 2nd ed. (Nicosia: Cyprus Research and Publishing Centre).

Theophanous, A. (1996) *The Political Economy of a Federal Cyprus* (Nicosia: Intercollege Press).

Theophanous, A. (2000) Prospects for solving the Cyprus problem and the role of the European Union, *Publius*, 30(1–2), pp. 217–246.

Theophanous, A. (2004) *The Cyprus Question and the EU – The Challenge and the Promise* (Nicosia: Intercollege Press).

TTC (2006) *Regional Tourism Strategy & Action Plan for the Free Famagusta Area, Tourism & Transport Consult International*, Dublin, Famagusta Chamber of Commerce.

Vassiliou, G., Antoniadou-Kyriakou, P., Partasides, C., Paschalis, C., Pophaides, Z. & Platis, S. (2003) *The Economics of the Solution Based on the Annan Plan*, Monograph, Nicosia.

Warner, J. (1999) North Cyprus: Tourism and the challenge of non-recognition, *Journal of Sustainable Tourism*, 7(2), pp. 128–145.

Webster, C. & Lordos, A. (2006) Who supported the Annan plan? An exploratory statistical analysis of the demographic, political, and attitudinal correlates, *The Cyprus Review*, 18(1), pp. 13–35.

Webster, C. & Timothy, D. (2006) Traveling to the 'other side': The occupied zone and Greek Cypriot views on crossing the Green Line, *Tourism Geographies*, 8(2), pp. 163–181.

Webster, C. (2005a) Greek Cypriots perspectives on interacting with Turkish Cypriots, *The Cyprus Review*, 17(1), pp. 123–132.

Webster, C. (2005b) Division or unification in Cyprus? The role of demographics, attitudes and party inclination on Greek Cypriot preferences for a solution to the cyprus problem, *Ethnopolitics*, 4(3), pp. 299–309.

Winnett, J. (2008) Tourists don't want a Cyprus problem lecture, *Sunday Mail*, April 6, Nicosia, p. 16.

World Bank (2006) *Sustainability and Sources of Economic Growth in the Northern Part of Cyprus: Vol. I. Economic Assessment* (Washington, DC: Poverty Reduction and Economic Management Unit, Europe and Central Asia Region).

Yildizian, A. & Ehteshami, A. (2004) Ethnic conflict in Cyprus and the contact hypothesis: An empirical investigation. Paper presented at 1st Global Conference: Evil, Law and the State: Issues in State Power and Violence, July 14–17, Oxford, Mansfield College.

Zetter, R. (1994) The Greek-Cypriot refugees: Perceptions of return under conditions of protracted exile, *International Migration Review*, 28(2), pp. 307–322.

Public Policies and Development of the Tourism Industry in the Aegean Region

YAPRAK GÜLCAN, YEŞİM KUŞTEPELİ & SEDEF AKGÜNGÖR

Department of Economics, Faculty of Business, Dokuz Eylül University

ABSTRACT *Evidence in developing countries, especially in the Mediterranean basin, shows that the tourism sector has an important role in regional industrialization and economic growth [Tosun, C., Timothy, D. & Öztürk, Y. (2003) Tourism growth, national development, regional inequality in Turkey, Journal of Sustainable Tourism, 11(2–3), pp. 133–161]. Turkey has been successful in developing resort areas and attracting large number of tourists. The tourism sector is a highpoint industry and a crucial public policy area for the Mediterranean and Aegean Regions. The article has two aims: (1) to determine the significance of the tourism industry in the Aegean Region in Turkey by looking at specialization patterns in economic activities across the country and to identify the provinces of the region within which tourism is a highpoint industry and (2) to explore whether public investment in tourism in the Aegean Region has an impact on the value added created by the tourism industry. A comparison of regional structures of the regions reveals that 30% of tourism licensed accommodation establishments are located in the Aegean Region. The results from the location quotient estimates for 1995 and 2001 reveal that the Aegean Region is highly specialized in the tourism industry, particularly when the spatial distribution of the hotels is observed. Value added created by hotels of the Aegean Region is higher than the country average as well. In addition, the econometric model shows that the regional value added created by the tourism sector between 1995 and 2001 is significantly enhanced by public policies that focus on the sector.*

1. Introduction

The tourism industry is considered to be among the major sources of regional economic growth and job creation. Regions and local authorities play a key role in the formulation of policy and development of tourism (OECD Programme of Research on Road Transport and Intermodal Linkages, 2000). The tourism sector generates jobs not only in its own sector but also via indirect and induced effects in connected sectors such as financial services, retailing and telecommunications. Tourism has a positive multiplier effect on regional employment and income, but the magnitude of regional multiplier varies according to the characteristics of each individual region (Constantin, 2000; Constantin & Constantin, 2007). As tourism and regional development are closely linked, regions and local authorities play key roles in the formulation of policy and the development of tourism. Thus, coordination between local authorities increases the benefits of policies such as large-scale infrastructure projects (Constantin, 2000; Unutmaz, 2000; Khadaroo & Seetanah, 2007).

Evidence in developing countries, especially in the Mediterranean basin, shows that the tourism sector has an important role in regional industrialization and economic growth (Çımat & Bahar, 2003; Tosun et al., 2003). Turkey has been successful in developing resort areas and attracting large number of tourists. The tourism sector is a highpoint industry and a crucial public policy area for the Mediterranean and Aegean Regions in Turkey.

Close link between regional development and specialization is based on the idea that success in economic development depends in part on the development of localized concentrations of industries (Falcıoğlu & Akgüngör, 2008). The idea that specialization of a region creates a synergy to enhance the region's success in economic development dates back to Marshall's concept of polarization theory (Myrdal, 1957; Hirschman, 1958) and further elaborated by new economic geography theory (Krugman, 1991; Fujita et al., 1999). The underlying idea is that competitive advantage lies outside the boundaries of the firms and those interactions across the firms and institutions affect the region's economic performance through diffusion of technology, transfer of innovation, skills and knowledge (Akgüngör, 2006).

The article has two major objectives: to determine the significance of the tourism industry in the Aegean Region in general and to identify the patterns of specialization of the tourism industry within the region. The second objective is to explore whether public investment in tourism in the Aegean Region has an impact on the value added created by the tourism industry.

It is evident that 30% of tourism licensed accommodation establishments are located in the Aegean Region (Republic of Turkey, Ministry of Culture and Tourism, 2007). This article aims to build upon this knowledge by exploring the patterns of industrial specialization of the regions across the country and the provinces across the Aegean Region. Such knowledge would be a guide for public policymakers in making decisions with respect to allocations of public budget for tourism-related industries. The article also provides insight with regard to returns to public investments into the tourism sector.

The results of this study is therefore, significantly important in the sense that they will reveal for which provinces in the Aegean Region tourism is a promising industry for regional development. The knowledge will further give accurate directions and implications for public policies towards the tourism industry.

The rest of the article is organized as follows. Section 2 explains the conceptual framework and Section 3 provides the empirical analysis including data, method and the empirical estimation results. Finally, Section 4 concludes.

2. Conceptual Framework

The spatial distribution of economic activity among regions is an important determinant of regional economic development. According to the new classical theory, regional development and concentration are directly related to the benefits of locating in areas endowed with natural advantages (Guerrero & Sero, 1997; Fujita, 1998; Manuel Acosta & Daniel Coronado, 1998; Ottaviano & Puga, 1998).

The theory of cumulative causation (Myrdal, 1957; Kaldor, 1970, 1985) predicts a pattern of uneven regional development in contrast to the neoclassical story of per capita income convergence across regions. The attractiveness of higher incomes in the region is reinforced by processes of increasing returns. Many rural development economists accept parts of both the neoclassical and cumulative causation stories of regional economic change, despite conflicting assumptions and conclusions between the two theories. The functional forms used in neoclassical theory to represent production and consumption behaviour are not perfectly useful to explain complex interactions such as intra-industry networking and the formation of public–private partnerships to spur economic development. To explain such interactions, rural, urban and regional development economists have long made use of the notion of agglomeration economies (Kraybill, 1999).

Agglomeration economies, by definition, describe the benefits that firms obtain when they locate close to each other. When more related firms are clustered together, due to greater specialization and division of labour, the cost of production is lower and the market that the firms sell into is greater (Blair, 1995). This is referred to as *localization economies* or *Marshallian externalities* in the literature. Localization economies are also defined as the externalities stemming from the geographical proximity of related actors and interpreted as the spatial meaning of increasing returns (Boschma & Lambooy, 1999). In this sense, agglomeration economies play a crucial role in the explanation of how spatial concentration comes about (Lambooy, 1986; Harrison *et al.*, 1996; Swann & Prevezer, 1996). The bigger the agglomerations, the more firms may benefit from a wider range of business services, a greater variety of potential suppliers and more specialized buyers, a larger and more diversified pool of (skilled and low-cost) labour, etc. (Arthur, 1994).

The new growth literature and the new economic geography theory, with emphasis on knowledge generation and adoption, are seen to be relevant for studying local economic growth (Glaeser *et al.*, 1992). They provide rigorous foundations for cumulative growth concepts that have long been the subject of non-formal theorizing by regional development analysts. Two common features of these theories are increasing returns (internal and external) and imperfect competition. Endogenous growth theory explains long-run growth as the result of investment in knowledge or human capital (Romer, 1986; Lucas, 1998), whereas the new economic geography theory is a general equilibrium framework in which spatial structure interacts with industrial structure to determine the location of firms and workers (Krugman, 1991). Interregional factor flows reinforced by increasing returns form the dynamics of these models and the processes of cumulative causation (growth and decline through factor mobility cumulatively reinforced by increasing returns).

The simple version of the economic geography model shows that with an exogenous increase in real wages, workers are attracted to the region and thus regional output increases, which in turn gives rise to agglomeration economies. The increase in consumer utility due to agglomeration economies attracts more workers. The principle of cumulative causation is observed when firms or regions that are successful in differentiating their products gain market power and are able to achieve lower average costs with increased scale (Kilkenny, 1999).

Jianyong (2007) examines how industrial agglomeration improves regional labour productivity in the case of China. Agglomeration is defined as the quantity of employment of non-agricultural industry in one unit area of land. The study provides evidence that the concentration on non-agricultural industry will significantly increase labour productivity in China. The promotion of non-agricultural employment density to labour productivity is agglomeration effect which in turn affects regional income inequality. The policy implication of the article is that regional government should make full use of locally increasing returns of manufacturing and service industry to increase the labour productivity by urbanization and industrialization.

For effective regional economic policies, it is crucial to understand and analyse the processes of urbanization and changing economic geography of countries and cities. The contributions of regional policies and especially of public infrastructure investments in shaping the location of economic activities and thereby promoting development stems out be a considerable challenge for policymakers. (Henderson *et al.*, 2001; Morgenroth, 2003)

Glasmeier (1999) stresses the importance of public-sector programmes by addressing the intersections between territory-based regional industrial development programmes and the challenges faced by firms in the emerging information-based economy. The main point is that sectoral approaches should be broadened to incorporate a more complex understanding of how information-based competition is altering the environment for both citizens and the business community (Malmberg & Maskell, 1999).

This article builds on the assumption offered by the new economic geography theory which points out the importance of local markets and horizontal and vertical production relations between firms (Venables, 1996; Falcıoğlu, 2007). It is accepted that geographic location and concentration are of foremost importance for tourism development and regional advantage (Braun *et al.*, 2005). Being familiar with the region's key industries allows the regions to be familiar with how the industries function and to be able to appreciate their needs and concerns. Knowing the region's key industries is informative in assessing factor conditions, home demand, supporting industries and industry rivalry all of which are components of local competitiveness (Porter, 2000).

In addition, successful clustering of the tourism activity and the value added created by the tourism industry depend not only on natural advantages but also on public policies. Public policies towards support for tourism are crucial in enhancing the value added created by the tourism industry and thus on regional development (OECD Programme of Research on Road Transport and Intermodal Linkages, 2000; Khadaroo & Seetanah, 2007).

3. Empirical Analysis

3.1 *Data*

The definition of tourism-related activities and the measurement of tourism employment cover a broad range of economic activities. Despite its importance, the measurement of the size of employment of tourism still needs to be defined precisely and consistently (Han & Fang, 1997). Drawing a boundary between the activities where tourism begins and ends is difficult. Although there have been efforts to reduce ambiguities related to boundaries regarding tourism, a consensus still needs to be reached (OECD Programme of Research on Road Transport and Intermodal Linkages, 2000). This study pursues the approach developed by OECD and also adopted by Association of Turkish Travel Agencies within which tourism-related economic activities are defined.[1,2]

Data for the tourism-related activities (as explained above) exist at the national level for Turkey. However, data at the regional level are unfortunately limited in coverage.

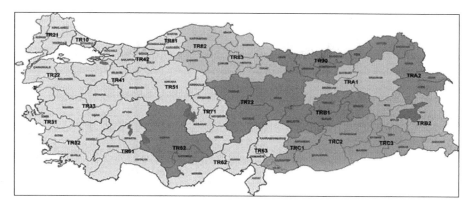

Figure 1. Turkey with 26 NUTS2 and 81 NUTS3 regions
Source: Turkish State Planning Organization (www.dpt.gov.tr).

The only regional data relevant to the tourism-related activities are related to hotels and restaurants (ISIC Rev 3, Codes 5510: hotels, motels, boarding houses, camping sites and other lodging places and 5520: restaurant, cafe, bar and other eating and drinking places). Therefore, ISIC Rev 3: Codes 5510 and 5520 are used as a proxy to measure tourism employment for the regions in Turkey.

Similar limitation problem persists in exploring the role and significance of tourism activities among others in a region's economy. In an effort to understand the significance of tourism-related economic activities, a common approach is to compare a region's tourism employment in a region's total employment. However, among all economic activities defined by United Nations, only some components of "Mining and quarrying (sections 10 through 14)" and "Manufacturing (sections 15 through 37)" exist at the regional level for Turkey. Other economic activities are not available at the regional employment data set. As a result, total regional employment is proxied by the sum of the employment of all or some subsectors of "hotels and restaurants", "mining and quarrying" and "manufacturing" as elaborated above.

There are 26 NUTS2 and 81 NUTS3 regions in Turkey as demonstrated in Figure 1. The Aegean Region is composed of three NUTS2 regions (TR 31, TR 32 and TR 33) and eight NUTS3 regions or provinces (Afyon, Aydın, Denizli, İzmir, Kütahya, Manisa, Muğla, Uşak), as can be seen in Figure 2.

3.2 *Method*

3.2.1 *Exploring regions' key industries*

To investigate the significance of tourism-related activities, the production structure and highpoint economic activities of NUTS2 regions across Turkey are compared. Then, the NUTS3 regions located in Aegean Region are analysed from the perspective of the potential of the tourism industry for regional development in order to identify current challenges and opportunities for sound public policies.

The following three ratios are used to measure the spatial structure of the role of economic activities across the NUTS2 and NUTS3 regions: (1) location quotient (LQ) (using employment as a unit of observation),[3] (2) LQ (using value added as a unit of observation)

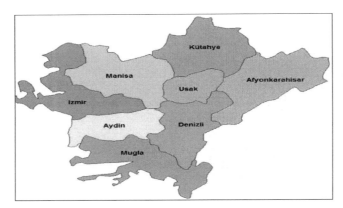

Figure 2. The Aegean Region of Turkey with eight provinces
Source: www.wikipedia.org.

and (3) value added per employment of industry *i* in the region relative to value added per employment of industry *i* in the nation.

In calculating these ratios, data on employment and the value added for the provinces for all economic activities in the Aegean Region for 1995 and 2001 are used. Available data at the NUTS3 level broken down into ISIC Rev 3 economic activities allow us to use time series data for the period between 1995 and 2001. To remain consistent in annual observations, we cannot extend the time series for the years after 2001.

3.2.2 *Exploring the relationship between public investment and value added in the tourism industry*

The econometric model through the use of a panel data analysis for eight provinces of the Aegean Region is a production function where the dependent variable is the value added of hotels (VAH) between the years 1995 and 2001. The model contains two different capacity measures for the hotels: number of beds (BED) and number of rooms (ROOM), which are used to proxy physical capital (Khadaroo & Seetanah, 2007). Nominal GDP per capita (GDP) is used to measure the effect on income on the value added of hotels. The average number of employees (EMP) in hotels is the human capital side of production function. This measure can also help to investigate the productivity of hotel employees. The main purpose of the econometric analysis is represented with public investments on tourism (PINTO) and public investment on tourism and communication (PINTC). The model is shown in the following equation:

$$VAH_{it} = \beta_0 + \beta_1 GDP_{it} + \beta_2 BED_{it}(ROOM_{it}) + \beta_3 EMP_{it} + \beta_4 PINTO_{it} + \beta_5 PINTC_{it} + \epsilon_{it}$$

where ϵ is the error term and "*i*" corresponds to the provinces in the Aegean Region. β_4 and β_5 are expected to be positive.

In the estimation of the equation above, the variables PINTO and PINTC are used interchangeably in three specifications. The first specification considers both PINTO and PINTC, whereas the second entails only PINTO and the third includes only PINTC.

In addition, the capacity measures BED and ROOM are considered separately in the estimations, but as the results are almost identical, the ones only with ROOM are reported. To control for heteroscedasticity, all regressions with fixed cross-section effects and White cross-section standard errors and covariance include an autoregressive term (AR(1)), which is the lagged value of the dependent variable).

3.3 *Results*

3.3.1 *Highpoint industries in the regions*
To search for the highpoint industries across the NUTS2 regions, the LQs for the 1995 and 2001 periods are compared (Tables 1 and 2). The results reveal that the three highest LQs for the hotels are at TR32 (Aydın, Denizli, Muğla), TR61 (Antalya, Isparta, Burdur) and TRA2 (Ağrı, Kars, Iğdır, Ardahan). With employment as a unit of observation, the three highest LQs for restaurants in 1995 are at TR33 (Manisa, Afyon, Kütahya, Uşak), TR51 (Ankara) and TR71 Kırıkkale, Aksaray, Niğde, Nevşehir, Kırşehir). In 2001, TR10 (İstanbul) replaced TR33, revealing that restaurant business in İstanbul has become a highpoint industry. Similar results prevail when the LQs are calculated with value added as a unit of observation, except with the exception of TR32 (Aydın, Denizli, Muğla) replacing TR33 (Manisa, Afyon, Kütahya, Uşak) in 2001 and TR10 (İstanbul) being the region with fourth largest LQ coefficient.

With respect to the geographic location of other economic activities, Eastern Anatolia regions have the highest LQs for mining both in 1995 and 2001. The regions where mining is considered to be a highpoint industry are TRA2 (Ağrı, Kars, Ardahan), TRC1 (Gaziantep, Adıyaman, Kilis), TRC3 (Mardin, Batman, Şırnak, Siirt), TRA1 (Arzurum, Erzincan, Bayburt) and TR81 (Zonguldak, Karabük, Bartın).

Manufacturing industry is most significant in TR42 (Kocaeli, Sakarya, Düzce, Bolu, Yalova), TR71 (Kırıkkale, Aksaray, Niğde, Nevşehir, Kırşehir) and TR90 (Trabzon, Ordu, Giresun, Rize, Artvin, Gümüşhane). As a result, when we compare the tourism sector (hotels and restaurants) with other industries (mining and manufacturing) across the NUTS2 regions of Turkey, the Aegean Region's provinces (Aydın, Denizli, Muğla, Manisa, Afyon, Kütahya, Uşak) seem to have good potential for the tourism sector as a regional growth engine.

For the hotels, the provinces of the Aegean Region create higher value added than the value added created in the whole country. For restaurants, the results are noticeably different particularly in 2001 where the highest restaurant value added was created in Ankara and İstanbul. The Aegean Region's Aydın, Denizli and Muğla come after İstanbul and Ankara (Table 3).

Tables 4–6 report the LQ figures and the values added as a ratio of the country average for the Aegean Region's NUTS3 regions. The figures show that hotels in Aydın and Muğla are most prominent with respect to specialization and value added. Restaurant business is noteworthy in Afyon, İzmir and Muğla.

Despite being located in the same geographic region, the provinces of the Aegean Region of Turkey have differences with respect to the significance of the tourism in regions' overall economic activity. Such differences point out the necessity of implementing unique regional policies to enhance and support the role played by the tourism industry on the regional growth. Public policies to enhance the value added created by the tourism industry should be the focus of attention.

Table 1. LQs for the NUTS2 regions in Turkey (unit of observation: employment)

	Hotels		Restaurants		Mining		Manufacturing	
	1995	2001	1995	2001	1995	2001	1995	2001
TR10: İstanbul	0.816	0.841	1.824	*2.374*	0.116	0.074	1.079	1.060
TR21: Tekirdağ, Edirne, Kırklareli	0.703	1.226	NA	NA	2.406	2.280	3.221	3.266
TR22: Balıkesir, Çanakkale	2.694	2.710	NA	0.302	4.376	5.407	1.773	1.722
TR31: İzmir	0.727	0.629	1.351	1.118	0.182	0.192	1.083	1.090
TR32: Aydın, Denizli, Muğla	*15.667*	*11.147*	1.314	1.282	5.676	6.892	1.997	1.945
TR33: Manisa, Afyon, Kütahya, Uşak	1.522	2.969	*5.520*	0.960	12.386	14.746	3.431	3.418
TR41: Bursa, Eskişehir, Bilecik	0.590	0.790	1.250	0.459	1.932	1.948	3.257	3.326
TR42: Kocaeli, Sakarya, Düzce, Bolu, Yalova	2.303	2.019	1.898	0.142	1.603	2.411	4.328	*5.538*
TR51: Ankara	1.159	1.270	2.725	2.548	0.997	0.772	0.975	0.968
TR52: Konya, Karaman	0.279	0.413	0.443	0.319	0.672	4.176	2.234	2.034
TR61: Antalya, Isparta, Burdur	*14.084*	*10.630*	1.172	0.393	1.364	1.399	2.462	2.380
TR62: Adana, Mersin	1.672	2.034	1.241	0.868	0.723	0.889	2.136	2.087
TR63: Hatay, Kahramanmaraş, Osmaniye	0.383	0.418	0.240	0.794	4.433	5.204	1.911	3.139
TR71: Kırıkkale, Aksaray, Niğde, Nevşehir, Kırşehir	11.244	7.343	*7.949*	*9.279*	4.014	2.829	4.667	4.855
TR72: Kayseri, Sivas, Yozgat	0.102	0.973	0.615	0.172	10.604	11.178	2.559	2.688
TR81: Zonguldak, Karabük, Bartın	0.035	0.422	NA	NA	*20.075*	*23.265*	1.766	1.930
TR82: Kastamonu, Çankırı, Sinop	1.044	0.083	NA	NA	5.430	6.371	2.943	3.104
TR83: Samsun, Tokat, Çorum, Amasya	0.711	1.067	0.647	0.797	9.749	9.703	3.749	3.951
TR90: Trabzon, Ordu, Giresun, Rize, Artvin, Gümüşhane	2.765	6.684	0.354	1.200	13.872	22.603	5.586	4.875
TRA1: Erzurum, Erzincan, Bayburt	0.801	0.817	NA	0.733	9.625	25.253	2.603	1.746
TRA2: Ağrı, Kars, Iğdır, Ardahan	*24.656*	*12.964*	NA	NA	36.402	18.595	NA	0.990
TRB1: Malatya, Elazığ, Bingöl, Tunceli	0.243	1.024	0.970	0.440	3.220	21.385	3.172	3.171
TRB2: Van, Muş, Bitlis, Hakkari	1.331	3.258	NA	NA	16.204	*35.071*	3.169	0.848
TRC1: Gaziantep, Adıyaman, Kilis	0.563	0.801	0.479	0.563	14.415	13.000	2.208	2.577
TRC2: Şanlıurfa, Diyarbakır	3.470	3.776	NA	NA	1.359	4.568	1.980	1.676
TRC3: Mardin, Batman, Şırnak, Siirt	2.221	0.899	NA	NA	21.347	53.526	2.678	1.019

Note: Italicized numbers show the highest LQs.

Table 2. LQs for the NUTS2 regions in Turkey (unit of observation: value added)

	Hotels		Restaurants		Mining		Manufacturing	
	1995	2001	1995	2001	1995	2001	1995	2001
TR10: İstanbul	1.216	1.223	2.470	2.897	0.176	0.144	1.047	1.023
TR21: Tekirdağ, Edirne, Kırklareli	0.576	0.745	NA	NA	1.608	0.963	3.153	3.280
TR22: Balıkesir, Çanakkale	1.579	1.312	NA	0.111	5.520	3.915	1.782	1.949
TR31: İzmir	0.448	0.260	0.632	0.477	0.136	0.106	1.070	1.102
TR32: Aydın, Denizli, Muğla	*24.255*	*21.696*	1.270	*5.071*	10.234	7.727	2.040	1.485
TR33: Manisa, Afyon, Kütahya, Uşak	1.718	2.756	*17.880*	1.832	18.672	18.418	3.060	3.288
TR41: Bursa, Eskişehir, Bilecik	0.277	0.462	0.822	0.474	3.345	4.205	3.044	3.115
TR42: Kocaeli, Sakarya, Düzce, Bolu, Yalova	1.751	1.046	1.063	0.026	1.325	2.796	*4.233*	*5.412*
TR51: Ankara	1.401	1.601	*3.512*	*3.117*	0.881	0.822	0.994	0.959
TR52: Konya, Karaman	0.190	0.438	0.294	0.402	1.342	3.864	2.088	2.008
TR61: Antalya, Isparta, Burdur	*34.938*	*15.265*	1.558	0.399	3.834	2.108	2.216	2.251
TR62: Adana, Mersin	0.370	0.783	0.990	0.962	0.552	0.790	2.135	2.154
TR63: Hatay, Kahramanmaraş, Osmaniye	0.345	0.277	0.565	0.443	7.393	5.286	1.685	3.066
TR71: Kırıkkale, Aksaray, Niğde, Nevşehir, Kırşehir	*12.403*	*11.075*	*20.495*	*10.228*	4.910	3.820	*4.807*	*4.635*
TR72: Kayseri, Sivas, Yozgat	0.059	0.367	1.093	0.206	17.486	14.515	2.117	2.545
TR81: Zonguldak, Karabük, Bartın	0.011	0.488	NA	NA	10.836	11.852	2.558	2.687
TR82: Kastamonu, Çankırı, Sinop	2.534	0.097	NA	NA	8.170	10.883	2.676	2.768
TR83: Samsun, Tokat, Çorum, Amasya	0.482	0.803	0.364	0.708	9.787	9.784	3.706	3.906
TR90: Trabzon, Ordu, Giresun, Rize, Artvin, Gümüşhane	1.375	4.609	0.298	1.324	18.644	43.293	*5.284*	*4.031*
TRA1: Erzurum, Erzincan, Bayburt	1.533	1.178	NA	2.865	23.400	34.135	1.695	1.379
TRA2: Ağrı, Kars, Iğdır, Ardahan	*30.867*	*18.085*	NA	NA	*55.494*	21.900	NA	0.959
TRB1: Malatya, Elazığ, Bingöl, Tunceli	0.084	0.408	0.576	0.321	6.561	24.347	2.837	3.120
TRB2: Van, Muş, Bitlis, Hakkari	0.806	7.097	NA	NA	19.904	*41.058*	3.033	0.615
TRC1: Gaziantep, Sdıyaman, Kilis	0.266	0.145	0.187	0.277	*29.481*	23.355	1.324	2.065
TRC2: Şanlıurfa, Diyarbakır	2.100	1.312	NA	NA	12.232	22.831	1.328	0.891
TRC3: Mardin, Batman, Şırnak, Siirt	0.209	0.088	NA	NA	39.212	*66.548*	1.775	0.781

Note: Italicized numbers show the highest LQs.

Table 3. Value added of the region as a ratio of value added of the country in Turkey

	Hotels		Restaurants		Mining		Manufacturing	
	1995	2001	1995	2001	1995	2001	1995	2001
TR10: İstanbul	1.709	1.667	*3.471*	*3.946*	0.247	0.196	1.471	1.393
TR21: Tekirdağ, Edirne, Kırklareli	0.483	0.554	NA	NA	2.858	1.682	*6.732*	*7.013*
TR22: Balıkesir, Çanakkale	1.122	1.014	NA	0.069	4.233	2.613	1.570	1.493
TR31: İzmir	1.201	0.686	1.694	1.261	0.366	0.280	2.868	2.912
TR32: Aydın, Denizli, Muğla	*14.209*	*13.239*	0.965	*3.182*	7.354	4.947	1.351	1.619
TR33: Manisa, Afyon, Kütahya, Uşak	0.531	0.979	*4.489*	0.741	*19.019*	*13.050*	1.899	2.082
TR41: Bursa, Eskişehir, Bilecik	0.572	0.833	1.628	0.795	5.036	6.360	*8.076*	6.234
TR42: Kocaeli, Sakarya, Düzce, Bolu, Yalova	*4.078*	*1.334*	2.520	0.178	2.115	3.085	*14.861*	*14.678*
TR51: Ankara	0.688	0.876	1.725	*1.705*	0.433	0.450	0.488	0.524
TR52: Konya, Karaman	0.081	0.142	0.125	0.131	0.571	1.256	0.843	0.653
TR61: Antalya, Isparta, Burdur	*12.684*	*13.206*	0.565	0.348	1.433	0.853	0.846	0.847
TR62: Adana, Mersin	0.448	0.669	1.095	0.758	0.645	0.679	2.566	2.004
TR63: Hatay, Kahramanmaraş, Osmaniye	0.059	0.054	0.085	0.092	2.647	1.182	0.400	0.566
TR71: Kırıkkale, Aksaray, Niğde, Nevşehir, Kırşehir	0.588	0.901	0.799	0.744	1.708	0.599	1.584	*4.487*
TR72: Kayseri, Sivas, Yozgat	0.048	0.100	0.219	0.167	2.833	3.175	0.946	1.162
TR81: Zonguldak, Karabük, Bartın	0.015	0.159	NA	NA	6.106	7.077	2.006	1.686
TR82: Kastamonu, Çankırı, Sinop	0.201	0.024	NA	NA	0.983	1.326	0.274	0.382
TR83: Samsun, Tokat, Çorum, Amasya	0.134	0.162	0.113	0.123	2.768	1.632	1.083	1.080
TR90: Trabzon, Ordu, Giresun, Rize, Artvin, Gümüşhane	0.297	0.836	0.041	0.230	4.643	*11.572*	0.865	0.901
TRA1: Erzurum, Erzincan, Bayburt	0.064	0.065	NA	0.159	8.237	1.979	0.126	0.115
TRA2: Ağrı, Kars, Iğdır, Ardahan	0.098	0.193	NA	NA	0.225	0.434	NA	0.106
TRB1: Malatya, Elazığ, Bingöl, Tunceli	0.034	0.171	0.227	0.065	1.862	0.848	0.751	0.673
TRB2: Van, Muş, Bitlis, Hakkari	0.036	0.137	NA	NA	0.123	0.050	0.109	0.012
TRC1: Gaziantep, Sdiyaman, Kilis	0.087	0.091	0.050	0.212	8.500	8.314	0.447	0.980
TRC2: Şanlıurfa, Diyarbakır	0.089	0.150	NA	NA	0.619	3.455	0.068	0.061
TRC3: Mardin, Batman, Şırnak, Siirt	0.042	0.011	NA	NA	8.582	*13.152*	0.541	0.097

Note: Italicized numbers show the highest LQs.

Table 4. LQs for the NUTS2 regions in the Aegean region (unit of observation: Employment)

	Hotels		Restaurants		Mining		Manufacturing	
	1995	2001	1995	2001	1995	2001	1995	2001
Afyon	1.099	2.644	*5.520*	0.775	1.124	1.001	0.943	0.839
Aydin	*5.203*	*4.237*	NA	NA	0.888	0.923	0.756	0.695
Denizli	0.561	0.177	0.114	0.174	0.571	0.373	*1.072*	*1.136*
Izmir	0.727	0.629	1.351	*1.118*	0.182	0.192	*1.083*	*1.090*
Kütahya	0.127	0.099	NA	NA	*8.259*	*10.404*	0.449	0.468
Manisa	0.062	0.064	NA	0.185	2.919	3.209	0.905	0.955
Muğla	*9.902*	*6.734*	1.201	1.108	*4.217*	*5.595*	0.169	0.115
Uşak	0.235	0.162	NA	NA	0.084	0.132	*1.134*	*1.156*

Note: Italicized numbers show the highest LQs.

Table 5. LQs for the NUTS2 regions in the Aegean region (unit of observation: value added)

	Hotels		Restaurants		Mining		Manufacturing	
	1995	2001	1995	2001	1995	2001	1995	2001
Afyon	1.398	2.428	*17.880*	1.711	2.409	1.055	0.866	0.898
Aydin	*9.782*	*10.226*	NA	NA	0.906	1.351	0.807	0.374
Denizli	0.547	0.483	0.084	0.255	0.372	0.521	*1.053*	*1.065*
Izmir	0.448	0.260	0.632	0.477	0.136	0.106	*1.070*	*1.102*
Kütahya	0.063	0.061	NA	NA	*13.057*	*14.344*	0.229	0.321
Manisa	0.030	0.040	NA	0.121	3.028	2.606	0.891	0.979
Muğla	*13.926*	*10.987*	1.186	*4.816*	8.956	5.856	0.179	0.046
Uşak	0.227	0.227	NA	NA	0.178	0.413	*1.074*	*1.089*

Note: Italicized numbers show the highest LQs.

Table 6. Value added of the region as a ratio of value added of the country in the Aegean region

	Hotels		Restaurants		Mining		Manufacturing	
	1995	2001	1995	2001	1995	2001	1995	2001
Afyon	0.351	0.827	*4.489*	0.583	0.605	0.360	0.217	0.306
Aydin	*3.274*	*6.105*	NA	NA	0.303	0.806	0.270	0.224
Denizli	0.492	0.620	0.075	0.327	0.335	0.669	0.947	*1.368*
Izmir	1.201	0.686	*1.694*	*1.261*	0.366	0.280	*2.868*	2.912
Kütahya	0.071	0.039	NA	NA	*14.683*	*9.179*	0.258	0.205
Manisa	0.037	0.052	NA	0.158	*3.675*	*3.400*	*1.081*	*1.277*
Muğla	*10.443*	*6.513*	0.890	2.855	*6.716*	*3.472*	0.135	0.027
Uşak	0.073	0.061	NA	NA	0.057	0.111	0.343	0.293

Note: Italicized numbers show the highest LQs.

3.3.2 *Public investment and tourism in the Aegean Region*

Having elaborated that the Aegean Region is highly specialized in the tourism sector, the next step is to investigate the connection between the value added created by the tourism industry and public investment in tourism in the Aegean Region. It is hypothesized that

Table 7. Public investment and tourism in the Aegean Region (1995–2001)

Variable	Specification 1	Specification 2	Specification 3
Constant	−6,807,574** (−1.777)	−7,068,309** (−1.971)	−1,168,979* (−3.003)
GDP	−0.001 (−0.054)	−5.72E−05 (−0.004)	−0.001 (−0.036)
ROOM	323.237 (0.422)	386.328 (0.443)	2513.981* (3.141)
EMP	−799.497 (−0.541)	−565.848 (−0.373)	−3686.261* (−3.057)
PINTO	*3.771* (3.573)*	*3.632* (3.808)*	
PINTC	0.011 (1.246)		−0.001 (−0.055)
AR(1)	1.523* (15.169)	1.538* (16.769)	1.563* (13.218)
R^2	0.99	0.99	0.98
F-statistic	270.19	295.98	180.03
Probability (F-statistic)	0.000	0.000	0.000
Durbin–Watson	1.998	2.021	1.765

Notes: The numbers in parentheses are *t*-values. Italicized numbers show the highest LQs.

*Statistical significance at 1%.

**Statistical significance at 10%.

there is a positive relationship between public policies towards tourism and the value added created by the tourism industry.

Table 7 reveals that GDP has a negative effect on the value added but the coefficient is very small in magnitude and is statistically insignificant. The number of rooms (ROOM) has a positive coefficient for all specifications; its effect is greater in magnitude and statistically significant at 1% when only PINTC is used for public investment measure in specification 3. This means that the capacity of the hotels in the cities of the Aegean Region could further be increased as it would increase the value added of the hotels. The coefficient of the average number of employees in hotels (EMP) has a negative sign all through; however, it is also greater in magnitude and statistically significant at 1% in specification 3. This result suggests that if more people are employed in the hotels, the value added of the hotels will decrease; that is to say, there is already enough employment in the hotels, more will lead to diminishing returns.

The hypothesis that public investment in tourism increases the value added of the hotels is confirmed by the coefficient of the variable PINTO which is statistically significant in models 1 and 2. Public investments in tourism and communication turn out to be insignificant in addition to its different signs for specifications 1 and 3.

4. Concluding Remarks

Following the idea that there is a close link between localization of economic activity and economic development of a region, the tourism sector is considered to be a potential impetus for regional growth particularly for the coastal areas of the Aegean Region. The article focuses on the significance of the tourism sector in the Aegean Region in comparison with the rest of the nation.

The results from LQ estimations reveal that the three highest LQs for the hotels are at TR32 (Aydın, Denizli, Muğla), TR61 (Antalya, Isparta, Burdur) and TRA2 (Ağrı, Kars, Iğdır, Ardahan). The results are similar when the LQs are calculated with the values added as a unit of observation, with the exception of TR32 (Aydın, Denizli, Muğla) replacing TR33 (Manisa, Afyon, Kütahya, Uşak) in 2001 and TR10 (İstanbul) being the region with fourth largest LQ coefficient. Thus, the Aegean Region is found to be highly specialized in the tourism industry. In addition, the value added created by hotels of the Aegean Region is higher than the country average as well. For restaurants, the results are distinctly different where the highest restaurant value added was created in İstanbul. The second highest value added ratio is the Aegean Region's Aydın, Denizli and Muğla followed by Ankara and İzmir. It is evident that a higher value added created by the localized industry in the region contributes to regional development.

The results from the econometric model assert the hypothesis that public investments in tourism are significant tools to create higher value added in the region. The positive relationship between public investment in tourism and the value added created by the tourism sector indicates that the regional value added is significantly enhanced by public policies that focus on the sector.

Notes

1. The OECD definition includes the industries whose ISIC Rev 3 codes are listed as follows: 55 (hotels and restaurants); 60 (land transport); 61 (water transport); 62 (air transport); 6304 (travel agencies, tour operators and tour guides), 7701 (car rental); 92 (recreational, cultural and sporting facilities); other tourism-related activities (see OECD Programme of Research on Road Transport and Intermodal Linkages, 2000, Tourism Satellite Account).
2. According to the Association of Turkish Travel Agencies (TURSAB), the tourism industry covers (1) hotels (ISIC Rev 3 codes of 551001, 551002, 551003, 551004, 551005, 551009, 551011, 551013, 551014); (2) restaurants (ISIC Rev 3 codes of 552001, 552002, 552003, 552004, 552005, 552006, 552007, 552008, 552011); (3) transportation (ISIC Rev 3 codes of 6021, 6022, 6110, 6210, 6220, 6303, 6304, 6309). (For details see http://www.tursab.org.tr/content/turkish/istatistikler/gostergeler/04istihdam.htm.)
3. LQ is a measure of the industry's concentration in an area relative to the rest of the nation. LQ= ((Industry's local employment (or value added))/(total local employment (or value added)))/((industry's national employment (or value added))/total national employment (or value added))). An LQ greater than 1 means that the cluster employs a greater share of the local workforce than it does nationally. LQ value greater than 1.25 is considered to be an initial evidence of regional specialization (for further information, see "Business Clusters in the UK" a report for the Department of Trade and Industry by a consortium led by Trends Business Research, February 2001).

References

Akgüngör, S. (2006) Geographic concentrations in Turkey's manufacturing industry: Identifying regional high-point clusters, *European Planning Studies*, 14(2), pp. 169–197.

Arthur, W. B. (1994) *Increasing Returns and Path Dependence in the Economy* (Ann Arbor, MI: University of Michigan Press).

Blair, J. P. (1995) *Local economic development: Analysis and practice* (Thousand Oaks, CA: Sage Publications).

Boschma, R. A. & Lambooy, J. G. (1999) Evolutionary economics and economic geography, *Journal of Evolutionary Economics*, 9(4), pp. 411–429.

Braun, P., McRae-Williams, P. & Lowe, J. (2005) Small business clustering: Accessing knowledge through local networks, in: *CRIC Cluster Conference 2005*, June 30–July 1 2005 (Ballarat: CRIC).

Çımat, A. & Bahar, O. (2003) Turizm Sektörünün Türkiye Ekonomisi İçindeki Yeri ve Önemi Üzerine Bir Değerlendirme, *Akdeniz İ.İ.B.F. Dergisi*, 6, pp. 1–18.

Constantin, D. L. (2000) Tourism and environmentally sustainable regional development: The case of Romania, in: *40th Congress of the European Regional Science Association*, 29 August–1 September 2000 (Vienna, Austria: European Regional Science Association).

Constantin, D. L. & Constantin, M. (2007) Strategies for cultural tourism, sustainability and regional develop-ment. A case study in Romania, in: *47th Congress of European Regional Science Association*, August 29–September 2 (Paris: European Regional Science Association).

Falcıoğlu, P. (2007) Spatial patterns of the Turkish manufacturing industry in the context of economic integration: An analysis for the post 1980 period, Ph.D. thesis, Işık University, Istanbul, Turkey.

Falcıoğlu, P. & Akgüngör, S. (2008) Regional specialisation and industrial concentration patterns in Turkish manufacturing industry: 1980–2000 period, *European Planning Studies*, 16(2), pp. 303–323.

Fujita, M. (1998) A monopolistic competition model of spatial aglomeration: Differentiated product approach, *Regional Science and Urban Economics*, 18(1), pp. 87–124.

Fujita, M., Krugman, P. R. & Venables, A. J. (1999) *The Spatial Economy: Cities, Regions and International Trade* (Cambridge, MA: MIT Press).

Glaeser, E., Kallal, H., Scheinkman, J. & Shleifer, A. (1992) Growth in cities, *Journal of Political Economy*, 100(6), pp. 1126–1152.

Glasmeier, A. K. (1999) Territory-based regional development policy and planning in a learning economy: The case of "real service centers" in industrial districts, *European Urban and Regional Studies*, 6(1), pp. 73–84.

Guerrero, D. C. & Sero, M. A. (1997) Spatial distribution of patents in Spain: Determining factors and conse-quences on regional development, *Regional Studies*, 31(4), pp. 381–390.

Han, X. & Fang, B. (1997) Measuring the size of tourism and its impact in an economy, *Statistical Journal of the UN Economic Commission for Europe*, 14(4), pp. 357–378.

Harrison, B., Kelley, M. R. & Gant, J. (1996) Innovative firm behaviour and local milieu: Exploring the intersec-tion of agglomeration, firm effects, and technological change, *Economic Geography*, 72(3), pp. 233–258.

Henderson, J. V., Shalizi, Z. & Venables, A. J. (2001) Geography and development, *Journal of Economic Geography*, 1(1), pp. 81–105.

Hirschman, A. (1958) *The Strategy of Economic Development* (New Haven, CT: Yale University Press).

Jianyong, F. (2007) Industrial agglomeration and difference of regional productivity, *Frontiers Economics China*, 2(3), pp. 346–361.

Kaldor, N. (1970) The case for regional policies, *Scottish Journal of Political Economy*, 17(3), pp. 337–348.

Kaldor, N. (1985) *Economics Without Equilibrium* (Cardiff: University College Cardiff Press).

Khadaroo, J. & Seetanah, B. (2007) Transport infrastructure and tourism development, *Annals of Tourism Research*, 34(4), pp. 1021–1032.

Kilkenny, M. (1999) New economic geography for low density places: Insights from Kaldor and Lancaster, in: *Conceptual Foundations of Economic Research in Rural Studies*, National Rural Studies Committee (NRSC), Western Rural Development Center, Oregon State University, January.

Kraybill, D. S. (1999) *Growth in Rural and Regional Economies*, Working paper, Columbus, Ohio, Department of Agricultural, Environmental, and Development Economics, The Ohio State University.

Krugman, P. (1991) Increasing returns and economic geography, *Journal of Political Economy*, 99(3), pp. 484–499.

Lambooy, J. G. (1986) Locational decisions and regional structure, in: J. H. P. Paelinck (Ed.) *Human Behaviour in Geographical Space*, pp. 149–165 (London: Gower).

Lucas, R. E., Jr (1998) On the mechanics of economic development, *Journal of Monetary Economics*, 22(1), pp. 3–42.

Malmberg, A. & Maskell, P. (1999) Localized learning and regional economic development, *Guest Editorial, European Urban and Regional Studies*, 6(1), pp. 5–8.

Manuel Acosta, S. & Daniel Coronado, G. (1998) The influence of regional location on the innovation activity of Spanish firms: A logit analysis, in: *ERSA Conference Papers ersa98p63* (Vienna, Austria: European Regional Science Association).

Ministry of Culture and Tourism (2007) *Tourism Strategy of Turkey—2023*, Publication Number: T.R. Ministry of Culture and Tourism Publications – 3090, Ankara: Ministry of Culture and Tourism Publications.

Morgenroth, E. (2003) *What Should Policy Makers Learn from Recent Advances in Growth Theory and New Economic Geography?* Papers from Economic and Social Research Institute (ESRI), No: WP150, Dublin: ESRI.

Myrdal, G. (1957) *Economic Theory and Underdeveloped Regions* (London: Duckworth & Co).

OECD Programme of Research on Road Transport and Intermodal Linkages (2000) *The Impact of Transport Infrastructure on Regional Development*, Abstract ITRD Number: E112022, organisation for Economic co-operation and Development (OECD).

Ottaviano, G. I. P. & Puga, D. (1998) Agglomeration in the global economy: A survey of the new economic geography, *World Economy*, 21(6), pp. 707–731.

Porter, M. E. (2000) Locations, clusters and company strategy, in: G. L. Clark, M. P. Feldman & M. S. Gentler (Eds) *The Oxford Handbook of Economic Geography*, pp. 253–274 (Oxford: Oxford University Press).

Romer, P. M. (1986) Increasing returns and long run growth, *Journal of Political Economy*, 94(5), pp. 1002–1037.

Swann, P. & Prevezer, M. (1996) A comparison of the dynamics of industrial clustering in computing and biotechnology, *Research Policy*, 25(7), pp. 1139–1157.

Tosun, C., Timothy, D. & Öztürk, Y. (2003) Tourism growth, national development, regional inequality in Turkey, *Journal of Sustainable Tourism*, 11(2–3), pp. 133–161.

Unutmaz, H. (2000) The definition of planning principles of Holiday Villages built in Turkey, in: *40th Congress of the European Regional Science Association*, August 29–September 1 (Vienna, Austria: European Regional Science Association).

Venables, A. J. (1996) Equilibrium locations of vertically linked industries, *International Economic Review*, 37(2), pp. 341–360.

An Empirical Analysis of the Determinants of International Tourism Demand: The Case of Izmir

A. ÖZLEM ÖNDER*, AYKAN CANDEMIR** & NEŞE KUMRAL*

*Department of Economics, Ege University, 35100 Izmir, Turkey, **Department of Business Administration, Ege University, 35100 Izmir, Turkey

ABSTRACT *Tourism has become an important sector in Turkey as a growing source of foreign exchange reserves and employment over the last two decades. After being one of the most important tourist destinations for decades, Izmir lost its relative importance after the 1990s. With its historical, cultural values and nature, Izmir still has a significant potential for tourism. Given the importance of this sector for Izmir, this paper investigates the factors affecting the international tourism demand in Izmir using the time series data between 1980 and 2005. The double logarithmic model is used in estimation. Real exchange rates, the GDP per capita of OECD countries, the GDP per capita of Izmir and the transportation public capital stock of Izmir are the variables used to explain Izmir's international tourist arrivals. The empirical results show that the prices and income of the tourist-generating country are the main determinants of the demand for tourism. Income and price elasticities are above 1. Local factors related to Izmir's level of development and the transportation public capital stock have no significant effect. Policy implications derivable from this study suggest that government should encourage alternative forms of tourism development besides mass tourism.*

1. Introduction

Turkey has become one of the most important tourism centres in the World, especially in the Mediterranean Region. As Turkey has a large variety of tourism facilities, it is expected that it will become the new tourist "giant" of the Mediterranean region in the near future. It is estimated that its rank will go up from the 11th place in 1980 to the 4th place until 2025 in the region in terms of international tourism (www.world-tourism.org).

International arrival figures were 23.34 million for Turkey in 2007. EU countries (except the new members in 2007) hold 50.25%, the Commonwealth of Independent

States (CIS) hold 20.6% and Eastern Europe countries hold 11.7% of the arrivals (www.tursab.org.tr).

Tourism has become an important sector in Turkey as a growing source of foreign exchange reserves and employment over the last two decades. Tourism constituted approximately 5% of the Turkish GDP and is the second most important source of foreign currency earnings (www.tuik.gov.tr). The contribution of tourism to the Turkish economy has also been stressed by some researchers (Gunduz & Hatemi, 2005; OECD, 2008).

When the historical background of tourism in Turkey is examined, one can say that the development of the tourism sector has merely depended on mass tourism and tourism plans have been prepared to promote coastal activities, namely sea–sand–sun (3S). Moreover, although Turkey has a high potential for tourism, it has not developed alternative modes of tourism depending on natural, cultural and traditional assets of the country.

Izmir, as one of the leading tourism destinations in Turkey, could not realize its potential after the 1990s. However, tourism is an important sector for the region in terms of employment and growth. Factors affecting the demand for international tourism in Turkey have been investigated by several researchers (see, for instance, Icoz *et al.*, 1998; Akal, 2004; Akis, 1998). However, there appears to be no study related to the determinants of international tourism demand as far as Izmir is concerned. This issue has gained importance especially to develop a regional tourism policy for Izmir. Therefore, the main aim of the study is to explore the determinants of tourism demand in Izmir.

The rest of the paper is organized as follows. The next section provides information about the tourism sector in Turkey and Izmir. Section 3 explains the theoretical model utilized. Section 4 gives detailed information about the data employed in the study. Section 5 features the estimates of the study. The final section underscores the main findings of the study and makes some policy recommendations.

2. Tourism in Izmir

As a strategic port and the third largest city of Turkey, Izmir presents its services to cultural tourism with its countless historical sites reaching to our days from prehistoric times, works and buildings, museums, typical Aegean cuisine, handicrafts, festivals, festivities, and other local cultural specialties, as well as offering its respectful participation in the belief of tourism with a large collection of sacred places.

Besides these, with its historical identity, beaches and sea, mountains and plateaus, thermal waters, macchia and red pine forests, Aegean agricultural products and soft climate, Izmir presents many unique opportunities to realize recreational activities and nature-compliant tourism types (see Pirnar, 2005, for details).

Despite the varieties in choices, it can be seen from Table 1 that Izmir is still a destination for traditional tourist-sending countries (www.tursab.org.tr). The composition of nationalities of incoming tourists to Turkey has changed in recent years since Turkey has become one of the top destinations for Russian tourists and the CIS countries (www.tursab.org.tr). Yet, Izmir cannot attract newly emerging tourist-sending countries.

In addition, after being one of the most important tourist destinations for decades, Izmir lost its importance after the 1990s. The continuous decrease in tourism share in and around Izmir is shown in Figure 1. In the last 25 years, Izmir has lost its share by 50% (i.e. from 8% to 4%).

Table 1. First four tourist sending countries in 2006–2007–2008 (Izmir, first 9 months)

	Number of arrivals			Percentage change	
	2006	2007	2008	2006–2007	2007–2008
Germany	181,472	193,663	203,604	6.72	5.13
Italy	80,201	105,763	120,615	31.87	14.04
France	76,201	78,303	85,865	2.76	9.66
Great Britain	52,249	67,730	76,117	29.63	12.38
Total	390,123	445,459	486,201	14.19	9.15

Source: Ministry of Culture and Tourism, http://www.izmirturizm.gov.tr/.

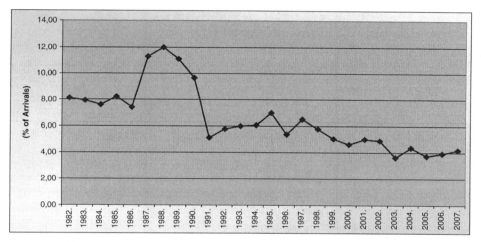

Figure 1. Share of Izmir in touristic activities (% of arrivals in Turkey)
Source: Ministry of Culture and Tourism, www.kultur.gov.tr.

The tourism industry has been growing in Turkey but Izmir was incapable of adapting to this growth. Figure 2 compares the share of Izmir with the other two important tourism destinations of Turkey—Antalya and Istanbul. As can be seen from the figure, the share of Izmir is declining through the years. The basic reason was that Southern Turkey had long and unoccupied seashore and became the "Turkish Riviera" with the governmental policies in the last 20 years. Consequently, the province of Antalya has become the star of Turkish Tourism with a 30% of share for arrivals. Istanbul, as the most important metropolitan region of Turkey, has increased its share through the years (Figure 2).[1]

Figure 3 presents the average length of stays in 2006. As can be seen from the figure, the average length of stay in Turkey is 4 days, where Antalya province has a 5-day average stay. Ankara and İstanbul have lower average lengths of stay due to business trips, congress tourism, etc. Izmir has an average length of stay slightly above 3 days due to its port and airport as well as having principal attractions such as the ancient city of Ephesus, etc.

Table 2 presents the average length of stay and occupancy rates in Izmir. The occupancy rate reveals important information about the present situation and the potential for tourism.

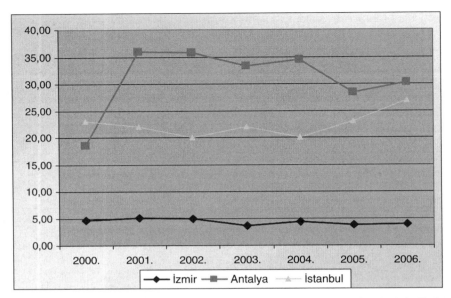

Figure 2. Share of Izmir, Antalya and Istanbul in touristic activities (% of arrivals in Turkey)
Source: Ministry of Culture and Tourism, www.kultur.gov.tr.

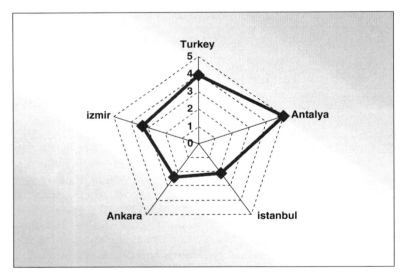

Figure 3. Average length of stay (days-2006)
Source: Ministry of Culture and Tourism, www.kultur.gov.tr.

The occupancy rate for Izmir, excluding camping sites, cannot exceed 50%, which shows that there is no need for more investment on new facilities, whereas the need for effective marketing efforts can obviously be seen. The highest rates are for four star hotels and holiday villages.

Table 2. Average length of stay (days) and occupancy rates in Izmir by type and class of establishment (Izmir 2006)

Type and class of establishment	Average length of stay			Occupancy rate (%)		
	Foreigner	Citizen	Total	Foreigner	Citizen	Total
Hotel						
5 Star	3.0	1.9	3.4	20.78	17.97	38.75
4 Star	3.9	1.5	2.6	31.26	15.58	46.84
3 Star	2.2	1.5	1.6	6.35	26.56	32.91
2 Star	2.8	1.7	1.9	6.93	27.13	34.06
1 Star	1.8	1.1	1.2	3.23	30.62	33.85
Special Licence	2.0	1.5	1.9	20.41	3.96	24.37
Thermal	–	–	–	–	–	–
Boutique	–	–	–	–	–	–
Apart	–	6.2	6.2	–	2.57	2.57
Total	3.1	1.7	2.1	17.46	20.69	38.14
Motel	4.4	4.6	4.5	13.61	14.66	28.27
Boarding house	7.3	2.7	2.9	1.48	12.43	13.91
Holiday village	5.9	3.5	4.2	17.59	27.16	44.75
Inn	–	–	–	–	–	–
Camping	10.4	13.8	12.5	24.39	51.76	76.15
Golf EST.	–	–	–	–	–	–
Training EST.	2.8	1.3	1.4	2.62	17.46	20.08
Tourism complex	–	–	–	–	–	–
Mountain house	–	–	–	–	–	–
Grand total	3.3	1.8	2.3	17.29	21.38	38.66

Source: Ministry of Culture and Tourism, www.kultur.gov.tr.

3. Model

Izmir cannot use its potential neither in terms of tourist arrivals, nor average length of stay. In order to investigate the issue further, we have estimated models for the determinants of tourism demand in Izmir and compared the results with the results of Antalya and İstanbul, the two other popular tourism regions in Turkey.

Tourism demand has been extensively investigated in the literature for different countries (see Crouch, 1994; Lim, 1997; Li *et al.*, 2005, for a survey). Income and relative prices are the frequently used variables. Tourism prices are in general not available. Exchange rates have been used as a proxy variable for price. Other exogenous variables are also considered, such as cost of transportation, and some attributes of the destination such as safety, infrastructure, etc. (see Crouch, 1994; Lim, 1997; Li *et al.*, 2005, for the use of additional exogenous variables).

Based on the literature, the international tourism demand model can be written as follows:

$$TOUR_t = \alpha + \beta_1 EXCH_t + \beta_2 GDPOPC_t + \beta_3 GDPPC_t + \beta_4 TRANSP_t + \varepsilon_t, \quad (1)$$

where $TOUR_t$ represents tourist arrivals, $EXCH_t$ is the real exchange rate, $GDPOPC_t$ is the per capita GDP of the OECD countries, $GDPPC_t$ represents the GDP per capita of Izmir, $TRANSP_t$ is the transportation public capital stock, ε_t is the error term and t is time.

The per capita GDP of the OECD countries are used as a proxy for income. It is expected that tourist arrivals increase as income increases (Usta, 2008, p. 95). The real exchange rate is defined as the price of the tourist-generating countries' currency in terms of the host countries' currency. The coefficient of the real exchange rate is expected to be negative. The GDP per capita of the region is an indicator of the level of economic development, which could promote tourist arrivals. The coefficient of the GDP per capita for Izmir is expected to be positive. Transportation infrastructure is expected to have a positive impact on tourism. If the tourism demand model is estimated in the log–log form, the coefficients could be interpreted as elasticities.

4. Data

In order to measure the tourism demand, we have used tourist arrivals. Another measure could be tourism receipts which were not available for Izmir. Data on tourist arrivals are obtained from the Turkish Statistical Institute (TURKSTAT). Data on real exchange rates are collected from the electronic delivery system of the Central Bank of the Republic of Turkey. Data on the GDP per capita of OECD countries based on purchasing power parity (PPP) are obtained from OECD data sets. Per capita income and transportation public capital stock data for Izmir are obtained from Önder *et al.* (2007). Except for the data on the GDP per capita for Izmir and the transportation capital stock, annual data from 1980 to 2005 were available. Data for the GDP per capita for Izmir and transportation capital stock were only available from 1980 to 2001. All the variables are used in a logarithmic form.

5. Estimation

Table 3 presents the results of the estimation in equation (1). The equation is estimated by the method of least squares (see Song & Witt, 2000, for different methods). The dependent

Table 3. Results of Model I 1980–2001 (dependent variable: TOUR)

	Coefficient	t-Ratio
Variable		
Constant	−8.952	−0.60
$EXCH_t$	−1.578	−3.59***
$GDPOPC_t$	2.117	3.25***
$GDPPC_t$	1.3946	0.77
$TRANSP_t$	−0.336	−0.72
Adjusted R^2	0.872	
Diagnostig tests		
Normality	0.45 (0.79)	
Autocorrelation χ^2 (1)	0.26 (0.61)	
Heteroscedasticity F (12.9)	0.67 (0.74)	

Notes: Normality is the Jarque–Bera test has Chi-squared distribution under null normality of residuals. Autocorrelation is a Lagrange multiplier test for first-order serial correlation. The White heteroscedasticity test has F statistic under the null of homoscedastic error. p values are in parenthesis.

***, **, * denotes significant at 1, 5, and 10 percent respectively.

Table 4. Results of Model II 1980–2005 (dependent variable: TOUR)

	Coefficient	t-ratio
Variable		
Constant	−0.342	−0.19
EXCH$_t$	−1.267	−4.20***
GDPOPC$_t$	1.956	14.36***
Adjusted R^2	0.891	
Diagnostic tests		
Normality	1.03 (0.60)	
Autocorrelation χ^2 (1)	0.17 (0.67)	
Heteroscedasticity F (5.20)	0.95 (0.46)	

Notes: Normality is the Jarque–Bera test has Chi-squared distribution under null normality of residuals. Autocorrelation is a Lagrange multiplier test for first-order serial correlation. The White heteroscedasticity test has F statistic under the null of homoscedastic error. p values are in parenthesis.
***, **, * denotes significant at 1, 5, and 10 percent respectively.

variable is the tourist arrivals and real exchange rate, GDP per capita of the OECD countries, GDP per capita of Izmir and the transportation capital stock of Izmir.

As can be seen from the table, the coefficients of real exchange rate and the GDP per capita of the OECD countries are as expected and significant. Price elasticity, −1.578 indicates a price elastic demand for international tourism. The results also show that income elasticity is above 2 indicating that tourism is a luxury good which is in line with the previous literature on tourism demand (see Eilat & Einav, 2004, for example) All the diagnostic tests are satisfactory.

The coefficient of the GDP per capita of Izmir and the transportation capital stock of Izmir are found to be insignificant, indicating that the local factors of Izmir do not have a significant effect on international tourist arrivals.

Table 5. Results of the model for Antalya and Istanbul 1980–2005 (dependent variable: TOUR)

	Antalya		Istanbul	
	Coefficient	t-Ratio	Coefficient	t-Ratio
Variable				
Constant	−35.732	−16.41***	−5.855	−2.48**
EXCH$_t$	−1.905	−5.004***	−0.033	−0.09
GDPOPC$_t$	5.942	34.63***	2.056	8.51***
Adjusted R^2	0.976			
Diagnostig tests				
Normality	1.35 (0.50)		34.40 (0.00)	
Autocorrelation χ^2 (1)	1.67 (0.19)		1.85 (0.17)	
Heteroscedasticity F (5.20)	2.55 (0.07)		0.31 (0.89)	

Notes: Normality is the Jarque–Bera test has Chi-squared distribution under null normality of residuals. Autocorrelation is a Lagrange multiplier test for first-order serial correlation. The White heteroscedasticity test has F statistic under the null of homoscedastic error. p values are in parenthesis.
***, **, * denotes significant at 1, 5, and 10 percent respectively.

We re-estimate the model by excluding these two insignificant variables. Table 4 presents the estimation results of the new model. Adjusted R^2 is higher in this model. The price and income elasticities are again above 1 and significant. This implies that income and price policies have a strong effect on the international tourism demand for Izmir. However, policies related to local factors are found to be ineffective.

In Table 5, we present the regression results for Istanbul and Antalya. It is interesting to note that the price and income elasticities are found much higher in Antalya province (−1.9 and 5.9, respectively). As far as Istanbul is concerned, elasticities are relatively lower (−0.03 and 2.05, respectively). In Antalya, the tourist arrivals are found highly sensitive to price movements and also to the income of the tourist-generating countries, since the province of Antalya has become the main centre of mass tourism for Turkey. However, for Istanbul, which has a different variety of tourism products such as business, conference, cultural, etc. elasticity figures were much lower. Another point to note is that the coefficient of price for Istanbul is found to be insignificant.

6. Conclusion

In this study, we estimated the international tourism demand for Izmir, which is an important tourism destination in Turkey. We used a double logarithmic model for the time series data between the years 1980 and 1995.

The results of the study show that prices and the income of the tourist-generating country are the main determinants of the demand for tourism, as income and price elasticities are above 1. On the other hand, local factors related to the development level of Izmir and the transportation public capital stock have no significant effect. These results imply that the tourism demand in Izmir mainly depends on the factors of tourism-generating countries. Local factors of Izmir have no significant effect on demand generation, which is typical for mass tourism-generating regions.

Izmir has a distinct place as an important centre for tourism, as it has a relatively developed infrastructure, and has rich natural, cultural and historical resources. Another advantage of the city is to be a close location to tourist-sending countries.

As being one of the leading tourism destinations at the beginning of modern tourism activities in Turkey, Izmir, having 7000 years of history, has a very significant potential for tourism with its location on the Aegean shore. The city also has a great potential regarding organic agriculture. Homeros wrote his world famous Iliad here, and the oldest temple for the goddess Athena was built in Izmir. Besides, Izmir was a home for the Hittites, legendary tribe of Amazons, Phrygians and many others.

Despite all this natural, historical and cultural richness, the city has not been able to utilize this potential. Thus, the demand for tourism is quite low and the city stayed at the back of many shining tourism destinations in the 1990s.

Policy implications derivable from this study suggest that the government should encourage alternative forms of tourism development besides mass tourism, via experience economy (including arts craft and design, artisan food alongside culinary, environmental, archaeological and the variants of cultural tourism) for Izmir. Agriculture and food industry depending on organic agriculture has a remarkable place in tourism policy in relation with experience economy. From this point of view, Izmir has a great potential and the government-started activities to form clusters for organic agriculture and considerable amount of support will be supplied. In such a cluster, culinary tourism can be developed, organic farms and a gourmet institute can be founded, world famous chefs and cooks can be educated and food festivals can be organized.

Besides organic agriculture, the richness of its 7000-year history can be utilized to present the visitors meaningful experiences (performances about daily living in ancient times, etc.). By this means, the number of visitors and revenues can be increased. Izmir can also be a leading city for health tourism with its thermal resources. The city can increase its activities with conferences, festivals, concerts, exhibitions, fairs, sports, and cultural events. In this respect, Izmir Development Agency may have an active role to promote sustainable tourism.

Note

1. Actually, tourist arrivals in Izmir increased from 481,620 in 2000 to 970,772 in 2007. However, the rate of growth has been relatively low compared with the growth rates in Antalya and Istanbul. Tourist arrivals in Antalya increased from 3,145,598 in 2000 to 7,689,061 in 2007 and tourist arrivals in Istanbul increased from 2,349,500 in 2000 to 6,453,582 in 2007.

References

Akal, M. (2004) Forecasting Turkey's revenues by ARMAX model, *Tourism Management*, 25(5), pp. 565–580.

Akis, S. (1998) A compact econometric model of tourism demand for Turkey, *Tourism Management*, 19(1), pp. 99–102.

Crouch, L. (1994) The study of international tourism demand: A survey of practice, *Journal of Travel Research*, 32(4), pp. 12–23.

Eilat, Y. & Einav, L. (2004) Determinants of international tourism: A three dimensional panel data analysis, *Applied Economics*, 36(12), pp. 1315–1326.

Gunduz, L. & Hatemi, J. A. (2005) Is the tourism-led growth hypothesis valid for Turkey, *Applied Economics Letters*, 12(8), pp. 499–504.

Icoz, O., Var, T. & Kozak, M. (1998) Tourism demand in Turkey, *Annals of Tourism Research*, 25(1), pp. 236–240.

Li, G., Song, H. & Witt, S. F. (2005) Recent developments in econometric modeling and forecasting, *Journal of Travel Research*, 44(1), pp. 82–89.

Lim, C. (1997) Review of international tourism demand models, *Annals of Tourism Research*, 24(4), pp. 835–849.

OECD (2008) *Tourism in OECD Countries 2008 Trends and Policies* (France: OECD Publications).

Önder, A. Ö., Deliktaş, E. & Karadağ, M. (2007) The effects of public capital stock on regional convergence in Turkey, in: *47th Congress of ERSA*, August 29–September 2, Paris, ERSA.

Pirnar, I. (2005) The importance of tourism for Izmir and suggestions for development (in Turkish), *Yonetim ve Ekonomi*, Celal Bayar University I.I.B.F. MANISA, 12(1), pp. 47–60.

Song, H. & Witt, S. F. (2000) *Tourism Demand Modeling and Forecasting: Modern Econometric Approaches* (Oxford, UK: Elsevier).

Usta, Ö. (2008) *Turizm Genel ve Yapısal Yaklasim* (Ankara: Detay Yayıncılık).

Index

Page numbers in *Italics* represent tables.
Page numbers in **Bold** represent figures.